W9-BUQ-490

INSIGHT POCKET GUIDE

AMSTERDAM

APA PUBLICATIONS
Part of the Langenscheidt Publishing Group
L

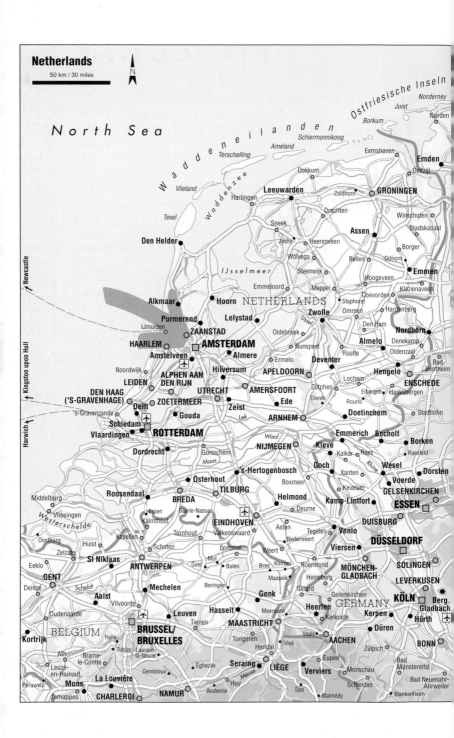

Welcome

This is one of 133 itinerary-based *Pocket Guides* produced by the editors of *Insight Guides*, whose books have set the standard for visual travel guides since 1970. With top-quality photography and authoritative recommendations, this guidebook – written by *Insight Guides'* expert on Amsterdam, George McDonald – brings you the very best of the city in a series of 18 tailor-made routes.

The guide begins with suggestions for three full-day walking itineraries linking the essential sights. It takes in diverse museums, churches, squares, shops and markets, with recommended stops at cafés, bars and restaurants. A further series of half-day and evening tours cover other interesting areas and aspects of the city, and three full-day, out-of-town excursions explore Haarlem and Zandvoort, the IJsselmeer and The Hague.

The itineraries and excursions are preceded by a chapter on the city's history and culture, and followed by sections on leisure activities – shopping, eating out, nightlife and a calendar of events. At the end of the guide a practical information section includes tips on getting around, money matters and dealing with emergencies, plus a list of recommended hotels and guesthouses at all price levels.

George McDonald, the author of this guide, is a freelance travel writer who caught the travel-writing bug as deputy editor of the inflight magazine of the Dutch airline KLM. One day he was editing local stories for a newspaper in Britain, the next he was paddling down the River Ganges for KLM. Most of his spare time was spent closer to home, however, in Amsterdam, exploring on foot, by tram, by bike, and in winter on skates, the marvellous city in which he lived.

He says of the city, 'Amsterdam is a state of mind as much as a real place,' and advises you to 'set your mental controls to "open-minded" and "ready for anything", and go.'

In addition to writing this *Insight Pocket Guide: Amsterdam*, the author has also written Insight Pocket Guides to Bruges and Brussels, cities he also knows well, and contributed to *Insight Guide: The Netherlands* and *Insight City Guide: Amsterdam*.

HISTORY AND CULTURE

From the early trading centre of Aemstelledamme through the Golden Age to the modern metropolis – an introduction to the forces that have shaped Amsterdam, one of Europe's most vibrant cities...**11**

CITY ITINERARIES

The first three tours link Amsterdam's essential sights. The subsequent 12 explore the rest of the city's most interesting districts and attractions.

1   The Golden-Age Canals follows the 16th- and 17th-century waterways that run through the city, taking in cafés, Anne Frank's house, museums and offbeat stores.......**23**

2   The Principal Squares begins with an elegant hotel breakfast before exploring a variety of districts, from the tranquil Spui to the bustle of the Kalverstraat area and finally to the hedonistic hub of Leidseplein.....................**27**

3   The Museum Quarter combines a tour of the city's premier museums with visits to the trendiest shopping streets and Amsterdam's most famous park **31**

4   The Old Centre (The Wallen) strolls through this characterful part of the city...**35**

5   The Zoo District visits the Botanical Garden, the refurbished Artis Zoo and the Tropenmuseum............**37**

6   The Harbour looks at the exuberant architecture of Centraal Station followed by a ferry trip across the IJ channel with views across Amsterdam harbour **39**

7   The Canals by Canal Bike offers an alternative, highly enjoyable, way to see the city – from the perfect vantage point of the water **42**

8   Amsterdam by Tram takes in many of the city centre's highlights and also provides an opportunity to see – and shop in – some outlying districts. **43**

9   By Bicycle along the River Amstel follows a tranquil riverside route out into the countryside to the pretty village of Ouderkerk aan de Amstel **45**

10   The Jordaan explores the atmospheric backstreets of Amsterdam's old working-class district.................**46**

11   The Jewish Quarter visits this distinctive district, taking in Rembrandt's house and the flea market........**48**

12   Amsterdamse Bos takes a picnic in the wooded park on the city's southern outskirts, where Amsterdammers go for a tranquil break. **49**

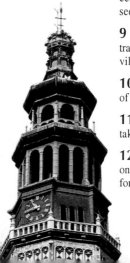

13 Leidseplein is an evening tour of the restaurants, bars, clubs, casino and bohemian haunts that form the city's pulsating nightlife centre **51**

14 Rembrandtplein, also an evening tour, offers a lively alternative to Leidseplein. The entertainment on offer around the brash square ranges from hip dance clubs to opera and ballet **53**

15 The Red-Light District samples the Oudezijds Voorburgwal area after dark **54**

EXCURSIONS

Three excursions to destinations within easy reach of Amsterdam.

1 Haarlem and Zandvoort takes the train west to explore two other facets of the country: Haarlem's quiet charm and Zandvoort's brassy seaside pleasures **57**

2 The IJsselmeer by Bike crosses the reclaimed land of the old Zuiderzee..**61**

3 The Hague catches a train to the elegant governmental seat of the Netherlands. After a look around the city it takes the tram to the coastal resort of Scheveningen **63**

LEISURE ACTIVITIES

What to buy, where to eat, and where to stay out late in Amsterdam...**67–76**

CALENDAR OF EVENTS

A guide to Amsterdam's festivals.................................**77**

PRACTICAL INFORMATION

All the background information you are likely to need for your stay, with a list of hand-picked hotels **79**

MAPS

Netherlands	...................**4**	*Jordaan*	.........................**47**
Amsterdam	.............**18–19**	*The Jewish Quarter*	.....**48**
Central Amsterdam	......**22**	*Haarlem*	.......................**58**
Museum Quarter	.........**32**	*IJsselmeer*	....................**61**
The Old Centre	...........**36**	*The Hague*	...................**63**
The Harbour	................**40**	*Transport Map*	.............**82**

CREDITS AND INDEX
pages **93–96**

Pages 2/3: Herengracht
Pages 8/9: the characteristic gabled architecture

History & Culture

Water is central to Amsterdam's history, geography and culture. The fishermen who first built their huts at the mouth of the River Amstel at the beginning of the 13th century earned a good living from the fertile fishing grounds of the Zuiderzee, although they and their families were at the mercy of wind and sea in that low-lying, swampy delta. Many must have lost their lives as frequent storm tides washed their primitive dwellings away. Yet the community flourished, particularly once a dam was built to hold the Zuiderzee at bay. A by-product of the dam was the creation of a good anchorage, at the point where Centraal Station now stands.

Named Aemstelledamme, the settlement soon expanded as a commodities market, to which influxes of Flemish weavers and Jewish merchants made considerable contributions. In 1275 – the year in which the city was officially founded – Count Floris V granted the people of Aemstelledamme toll-free passage on the waterways. This development encouraged further growth in trade. Ships unloaded cargoes of Baltic timber, salt and spices on what is now the Dam, and sailed away laden with cloth, furnishings and grain. In 1300, Guy van Avesnes, Duke of Hainaut, granted Aemstelledamme its town charter. Thirteen years later, Count Willem III of Holland took over the town from the Bishops of Utrecht who had hitherto controlled it. One more link in the commercial chain was forged in 1323, when Count Floris VI named Amsterdam as a toll-point for the import of beer. The city has lost none of its taste for this particular beverage, as a casual glance at the forest of Heineken and Amstel signs testifies, but in the 14th century beer was essential as an alternative to tainted water supplies.

The pattern of the city's history as a trading mecca was firmly established. Unfortunately the foundations of the city itself were not quite so grounded. Despite being built on waterlogged land, Amsterdam's wooden buildings were vulnerable to fire – and in 1452 most of them were engulfed by flames. In the wake of the fire, the City Fathers ordained, all new buildings would be made from stone. Today, the city has only two wooden houses.

A Phoenix from the Ashes

Amsterdam's golden age began towards the end of the 16th century, at a time when Calvinist Holland was fighting to win independence from Catholic Spain. It is not too far fetched to invoke comparisons with the Florence of the Renaissance or the Athens of Pericles. Amsterdam experienced a comparable burgeoning of art, culture, science and exploration. In the words of the British

Left: Amsterdam in the first half of the 17th century, when immigration boomed
Right: details of centuries-old gables show intriguing facets of the city's history

historian Simon Schama, 'There is perhaps no other example of a complete and highly original civilisation springing up in so short a time in so small a territory.' Although its lustre may have been dulled by the passage of four centuries, the glint of the golden age still shines.

The *grachtengordel,* the horseshoe of concentric canals that encloses the city centre, is the city's most timeless area. Names such as Prinsengracht (Princes' Canal), Herengracht (Gentlemen's Canal) and Keizersgracht (Emperor's Canal) are redolent of golden-age elegance. Work on the canals began in 1613, and the richly-gabled town houses represented the wealth that was a hallmark of the young Dutch Republic. Remnants of 17th-century life survive along this semicircle of patrician canals – in the adjacent crafts-men's community of the Jordaan; in the Dam, whose Stadhuis (Town Hall) was so imposing that the House of Orange turned it into a royal palace; and among the narrow canals and crooked houses of the *wallen* (the old centre), which today constitutes the city's notorious Red-Light District.

While the war with Spain ebbed and flowed, fresh ideas swept through the worlds of art, architecture and science, and explorers and merchants opened

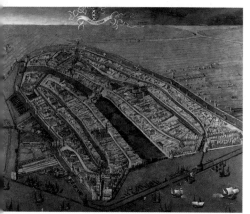

up new worlds. Amsterdam's widely shared prosperity gave rise to a large, confident middle class, whose members were eager to appreciate the finer things in life.

Population Explosion

In the first half of the 17th century, the city's population soared from 60,000 to nearly 220,000. In addition to accepting Catholics from countries that persecuted them for their beliefs, Amsterdam welcomed Protestant Huguenots from France, Walloons from Belgium, Lutherans from Ger-many and Jews from Germany and Portugal, and found that rarest of 16th-century virtues: tolerance. When religious revival was added, with Calvinism's triumph over the Inquisition and fossilised doctrines of Catholicism, the wonder was that the whole frothy mixture did not go to people's heads. Yet the Calvinist outlook was one of sober calculation, respectability and the determined heaping up of one florin upon another. Merchants gazing from their gabled houses at the forested masts of loading and unloading ships knew that God was in His heaven and that all was well with the world.

The Vereenigde Oostindische Compagnie (VOC), the United East India Company, which handled trade with the Orient, was founded in 1602, and its counterpart for the West Indies in 1621. The Bank of Amsterdam opened its doors in 1609 and the Amsterdam Stock Exchange in 1611. The long and difficult sea journeys to the country's far-flung possessions required stout ships, and the VOC's shipyard at Oostenburg in Amsterdam became the world's largest industrial complex. Today you can see a replica East India-man, as the vessels were called: the *Amsterdam* is tied to a quay at the

Above: the importance of waterways, seen in a map dating back more than 450 years

Scheepvaartmuseum (Maritime Museum), its tall masts a distinctive sight in the harbour. Ships such as the *Amsterdam* ploughed through the oceans, and returned laden with exotic products. One such expedition landed a hoard of late Ming Dynasty pottery, which gave birth to the Delftware (tin-glazed earthenware) industry.

The Golden Age

Profits from trade fuelled the fires of creativity, paying for the commissions that allowed members of the Artists' Guild to live in style. It was a creative period, not just in painting but also in sculpture and applied arts. Artists of the time were consciously trying to create a new art. They were moving away from rigid classical concepts and trying to achieve greater realism, to portray the dramatic moment. Frans Hals (1580–1666), who worked in Haarlem, just west of Amsterdam, founded the Dutch school of realism.

Undoubtedly the greatest artist of the period was Rembrandt van Rijn (1606–69), who was 25 in 1631 when he moved to Amsterdam from Leiden. For the following four decades, Rembrandt produced a series of masterworks – and apparently did not produce others with which he was later credited, to the emotional and financial distress of their owners. His best-known work, *The Night Watch* (1642), which hangs in the city's Rijksmuseum, illustrates a colourfully uniformed Amsterdam militia company. This

Above and Right: Rembrandt's *The Night Watch* and *Old Woman Reading a Lectionary*

work represents Rembrandt at the height of his powers in the heyday of the golden age. Amsterdam's own dramatic moment, however, did not last, and by the 18th century, the city's reservoir of inspiration, confidence and wealth was running dry.

In 1795 the Netherlands were invaded by the French, and in 1806 Napoleon installed his brother, Louis, as king of the Netherlands, with Amsterdam as his capital. Following Napoleon's exit from a Europe he had dominated for 20 years, the Low Countries' northern and southern provinces were united, though the latter achieved independence as Belgium in 1831.

World Wars

The country sided with neither the Allied nor Axis powers in World War I, but this neutrality made little impression on the Nazis, who invaded on

10 May 1940, during World War II. In a courageous act of defiance, the city's dockers led a general strike in protest at the first deportation of Amsterdam's Jews. The two-day strike has gone down in Dutch history as Amsterdam's 'day beyond praise'. The most famous Dutch victim of the Holocaust was Anne Frank, whose diary is a moving testament to the life of a Jewish family in hiding. Today, the Anne Frankhuis is one of the city's busiest tourist sites.

The country was still recovering from the long years of Nazi occupation when disaster struck. It is only due to Dutch engineering skill that the Netherlands has kept its head above water for the past 1,000 years, but in 1953 a combination of bad weather conditions sent the North Sea crashing through the sea defences in Zeeland. More than 1,800 people lost their lives. Canals, windmills, dikes and polders all tell the story of reclamation from the sea.

In the post-war period, Amsterdam developed a reputation for social liberalism with sex, drugs and squatting in the forefront. The Dutch, especially Amsterdammers, are renowned for their tolerance. But for all its progressive – or sinful, depending on your point of view – attitudes, more innocuous traditions continue to attract enormous numbers of visitors.

Amsterdam's Canals

The sea that has given Holland so much has also threatened much. An aircraft descending towards Amsterdam's Schiphol Airport has to descend further than would be the case at most other airports in the world because the runway is 7m (23 ft) below sea level. That it is not 7m under the North Sea is due to Dutch engineering skill, which has kept the country's collective head mostly above water for the last thousand years. Canals, windmills,

Above: in the 18th century Amsterdam was a thriving metropolis

dikes and polders all tell the story of a country pieced together at the expense of water. But believing is something else. A city such as Amsterdam seems timeless; its houses, shops, cafés and churches solid; its citizens very much at home. That waves should by rights lap where they stand seems unimaginable.

Amsterdam would not be the same without its canals. There might still be golden-age architecture, trams, brown cafés and museums, and perhaps its people would retain their iconoclastic outlook on life, but without the mirror of water, the city would be a shrunken glory. So have no qualms about stepping aboard a canal boat to view Amsterdam's delights from the best vantage point of all. You'll be forced to smile as you get your boarding picture snapped, then sit through a thumbnail-sketch history in several different languages. If you are particularly unlucky, you'll get doused with an anarchic pail of water while gliding under one of those romantic-looking bridges.

No matter. The canals are the best starting point in Amsterdam. Later, you can get mucky on a canal bike, hail a water taxi, or commandeer a passing rowing-boat. Amsterdammers might scoff as they watch the fleets of glass-topped boats, but secretly they are proud of them.

Tulips from Amsterdam

Holland's love affair with tulips dates back to 1594, when the botanist Carolus Clusius first cultivated the flower at the University of Leiden. From this modest beginnings has arisen an industry of truly astonishing proportions. In the 17th century fortunes were made and lost over a single bulb. Today the Bollenstreek (bulb district) south of Amsterdam is an enormous expanse of multi-hued tulip fields, and tulip lovers pour into Holland from all over the world. Tours by bus, boat, taxi, train, bicycle, on foot and from the sky all focus on the bulb fields. The gardens at Keukenhof in particular are frequently overrun, and the song *Tulips From Amsterdam* has entered the ranks of international folk cliché.

In the art world, Amsterdam has maintained the traditions of cutting-edge excellence established by the great masters of the 17th century. The post-World War II COBRA movement (an acronym of Copenhagen, Brussels and Amsterdam) was one of the 20th century's most influential. The COBRA museum in the Amsterdam suburb of Amstelveen pays tribute to this seminal, but short-lived, group of artists. In recent decades a new generation of Dutch artists – the likes of Arnold Mik and Marijke van Warmerdam – have come into their own, and a number of galleries in the city give a good overview of the state of contemporary Dutch art.

Right: *Flowers* by Hans Bollongier

The performing arts come into their own in the summer, when Amsterdam hosts music, dance and drama festivals in parks, squares, concert halls and even on the water. The highlight of the season is the Royal Concertgebouw Orchestra's concert in the Vondelpark. In June the Holland Festival incorporates a diverse array of opera, theatre and dance productions; at the end of August the Museumplein hosts a three-day fair, featuring theatre, music and dance, in preparation for the coming cultural season. Less formally, the Leidseplein has for years hosted buskers, mime artists and fire-eaters.

The Gay Capital

If the profusion of culture and arts events in the city is responsible for the nickname the 'capital of inspiration', a relatively long-standing tolerance of homosexuality has earned it the soubriquet the 'gay capital of Europe'. There are at least 35 gay bars, plus a couple of lesbian cafés, more than a dozen predominantly gay hotels and several gay dance clubs. The highlight of Amsterdam's gay calendar is the Gay Pride celebration that takes place on the first weekend of August.

A simple concept underlines everyday life in the city: the quest for *gezelligheid* – an enigmatic concept that is used to describe the special something that makes a place friendly, cosy and memorable. Although Amsterdam is one of Europe's great cities, it is intimate and accessible, with the ambience of a cosmopolitan village rather than a soulless metropolis. It is a city in which locals and visitors alike benefit from a glorious past while enjoying the fruits of a vibrant, tolerant present.

Above: a land of windmills
Left: traditional costume

HISTORY HIGHLIGHTS

circa 1200 Herring fishermen settle at the mouth of the River Amstel.

circa 1220 The first dam is built to hold back the tidal waters of the Zuiderzee at a settlement that becomes known as Aemstelledamme.

1275 Count Floris V exempts the people of Aemstelledamme from tolls on travel and trade.

1300 The Bishop of Utrecht grants Amsterdam its city charter.

1334 Work begins on the Oude Kerk, the city's first parish church.

1345 'Miracle of the Host' leads to Amsterdam becoming a place of pilgrimage.

1395 The city's first town hall is built on the Dam.

1400 Work starts on the Nieuwe Kerk.

1414 Amsterdam becomes Holland's biggest town, with a population of 12,000.

1452 Fire destroys most of the timber-built city.

1480 Defensive walls are built.

1535 Protestant Anabaptists occupy the town hall. The revolt is suppressed and Catholicism re-imposed.

1566 The city's first Calvinist church is established.

1576 Amsterdam, loyal to the Catholic King Philip II of Spain, is besieged by Prince William of Orange.

1578 The city surrenders and the churches and government are taken over by Calvinists.

1602 Establishment of the United East India Company, with its headquarters in Amsterdam.

1609 Bank of Amsterdam opens.

1611 Amsterdam Stock Exchange opens.

1613 Work on the *grachtengordel* – the Herengracht, Keizersgracht and Prinsengracht canals – begins.

1632 Establishment of the Athenaeum Illustre, which later became Amsterdam University.

1642 Rembrandt paints his most famous work *The Night Watch* (today exhibited in the Rijksmuseum.

1648 Work begins on new town hall.

1650 The city's population hits 220,000.

1745 Schools for needy children are established.

1795 Amsterdam becomes the capital of the pro-French Batavian Republic.

1806 Napoleon abolishes the republic and proclaims his brother Louis as king of the Netherlands, with Amsterdam as his capital.

1845 Pro-democracy riots lead to the establishment of a constitution.

1876 North Sea Canal opens.

1928 Amsterdam hosts the Olympics.

1940 Nazi Germany invades and occupies Holland.

1941 Workers, led by dockers, strike for two days in protest against the deportation of the city's Jews.

1942 Anne Frank and her family go into hiding.

1945 Amsterdam liberated by the Allies.

1965 Anti-establishment Provos win seats on the city council.

1966 Protesters disrupt the wedding of Princess Beatrix.

1992 Amsterdammers vote to curb car use in the city.

2000 The world's first same-sex marriage with a legal status identical to heterosexual matrimony takes place in Amsterdam.

2002 The euro becomes the country's official currency. The Passenger Terminal Amsterdam opens for cruise liners.

2003 Most of the Rijksmuseum closes for major renovation.

2004 After making a film critical of Islam, director Theo van Gogh is murdered in Amsterdam; anti-Muslim violence breaks out in the Netherlands.

2005 The new Muziekgebouw aan 't IJ concert hall opens on the city's redeveloping waterfront.

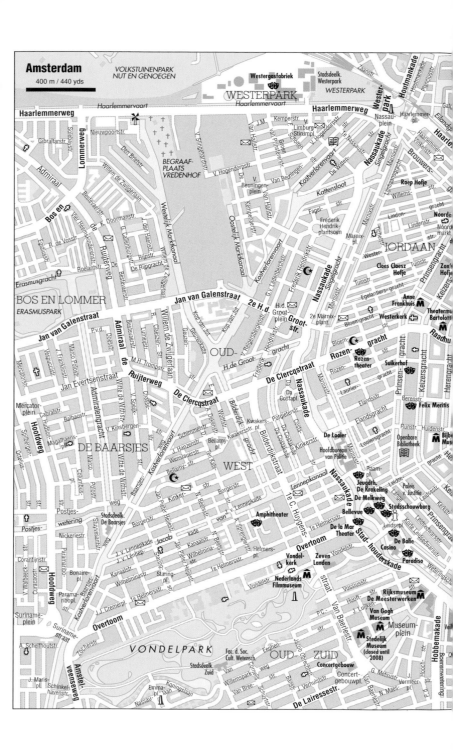

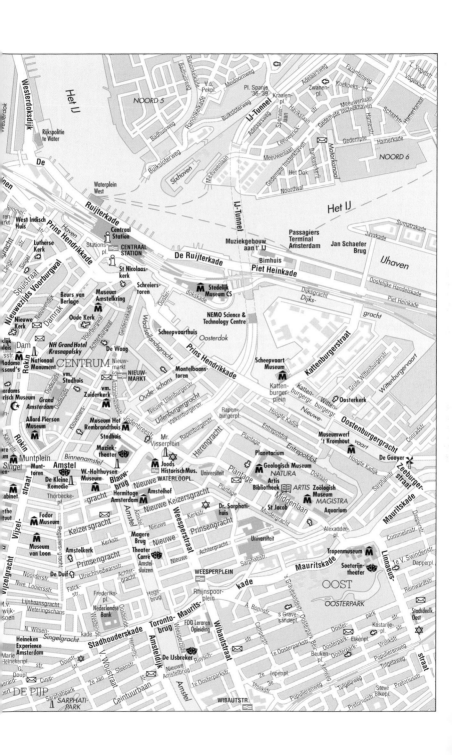

City Itineraries

The following itineraries consist of three full-day tours of Amsterdam's most important sights followed by a series of half-day and evening tours that explore other interesting areas and aspects of the city. After the city itineraries, three day-long, out-of-town excursions suggest visits to Haarlem and Zandvoort, the IJsselmeer and The Hague.

Most of the old city centre within the concentric circles of the golden-age canals is small and compact enough to be easily covered on foot. Amsterdammers think of the old city centre as a village. For travel beyond this neighbourhood, a combination of walking and riding on trams is highly recommended. Should you want to take a taxi, water taxi, canal bus, or the museum boat, bear in mind that all of these options are expensive. There is no better way of seeing this city of 165 canals than from one of its dozens of glass-topped canal boats. These excursions are justifiably very popular.

Hiring a car, or driving your own vehicle, is definitely not recommended. For one thing, Amsterdam has canals where other cities, Venice notwithstanding, have streets. Moreover, driving in the city has been limited since the municipality voted to stem the flow of cars some years ago. Parking is expensive, and the *dienst parkeerbeheer* (parking authority) takes its work very seriously. If you park illegally, you will invariably be caught; your car will be clamped or towed away, you will have to collect it from a car-pound out in the sticks, and then be obliged to pay a hefty fine to get it back.

Bicycles Abound

The bicycle is one of the most popular means of transport in Amsterdam – the city's 500,000 cyclists take advantage of the remarkably flat terrain. There are lots of places from which to hire a bike, and any number of bike lanes. Drawbacks to look out for include tram tracks – cross them at right angles to avoid getting your wheels caught; heavy traffic – locals think nothing of driving through red lights or on the tram tracks; and the potential for having your bike stolen – be sure to lock it and secure it to something solid whenever you leave it unattended.

Whatever your mode of transport, don't hesitate to venture off the beaten track and make your own discoveries. One delight of exploring Amsterdam is stumbling upon idiosyncratic details. These could be an unusually-shaped gable, an offbeat little store, a gaily-painted bicycle, or a sunken canal boat. Another attraction of this sophisticated city is the friendliness of its people, and the high level of English spoken, so don't be shy of striking up a conversation with strangers. This is a city that makes visitors welcome without even trying.

Left: café on the bank of the Singel canal
Right: one of the city's ornate gables

Central Amsterdam

200 m / 220 yds

- - - Itinerary 1
- - - Itinerary 2

1. THE GOLDEN-AGE CANALS *(see map, p22)*

This day-long itinerary follows the concentric semi-circle of 16th- and 17th-century canals – Singel, Herengracht, Keizersgracht and Prinsengracht. Highlights include the Anne Frankhuis, several museums and some offbeat stores. A substantial amount of walking is involved but there are lots of 'time out' possibilities along the way.

Begin west of Centraal Station at the junction of Haarlemmer Houttuinen and Korte Prinsengracht. If you are arriving from Centraal Station, you can either take the Opstapper minibus or walk to the starting point, along Prins Hendrikkade to Haarlemmer Houttuinen.

Three of the canals around which this itinerary is based are lasting testimony to the city's 17th-century golden age. It is unfortunate that the glories of that heyday have been tarnished by the less positive aspects of contemporary life – noise, pollution, parking problems, etc – but these minor annoyances do not completely break the connection with those Calvinist burghers who made the golden age shine.

Starting at the Korte Prinsengracht–Haarlemmer Houttuinen junction, walk along the narrow canal to the corner of **Brouwersgracht** (Brewers' Canal) and **Prinsengracht**. Note how all of the former brewery warehouses along Brouwersgrachthave been converted into expensive apartments. At the junction of the two canals are a couple of recommended spots, should you fancy a breakfast snack: **Café Tabac** (101 Brouwersgracht) and **'t Papeneiland** (2 Prinsengracht). Both are brown cafés (*bruine kroegen*) – old, traditional-style Dutch bars known for their colour, which comes from the wood being stained by centuries of smoke.

Market Square

Cross Brouwersgracht by the bridge here, then switch to the west (right) bank of Prinsengracht. The first stop is **Noordermarkt** and the **Noorderkerk** (North Church) that stands in the market square. On Saturday Noordermarkt hosts a **Bird Market** and, selling organically-grown produce, a **Farmers' Market**. On Monday morning there's a textiles and a second-hand market here. Some gables overlooking the square feature agricultural images – of cows, chickens and the like – that recall the square's historical role as a market. The Noorderkerk, designed by Hendrick de Keyser, the golden-age's master church builder, dates to 1623.

Continue along Prinsengracht to the bridge at Prinsenstraat, and turn left along this short street, which is lined with cafés and restaurants. Cross over the **Keizersgracht** bridge – note the houseboats moored on either side – onto Heerenstraat and continue to **Herengracht** before turning right along the canal. Continue to the **Theatermuseum** (168 Herengracht; Mon–Fri 11am–5pm, Sat and Sun 1–5pm; entrance fee). The museum occupies five

Right: all set for a pleasant canal cruise

adjacent canal houses, one of which, the **Bartolotti House** at No. 170–72, was constructed around 1618 by Pieter de Keyser, son of the great church architect Hendrick de Keyser, and is famous for its red-brick gable. In the museum you will find a wide variety of costumes, maquettes, masks, puppets, photographs, paintings and stage backdrops, covering all forms of theatre.

Anne Frank's House

Backtrack a few steps to Leliegracht, go up onto Prinsengracht and turn left to visit the **Anne Frankhuis** (263 Prinsengracht; Apr–Aug: daily 9am–9pm; Sept–Mar: daily 9am–7pm; tel: 556 7100; entrance fee), one of Amsterdam's most popular 'attractions'. This is the house in which the teenage Jewish diarist, Anne Frank (1929–45) hid with her family (and two other families) for more than two years during World War II before being captured by the Nazis, at whose hands she died of hunger and disease in

Bergen-Belsen concentration camp. Generally, the earlier you arrive the better, because the queues are sometimes very long. In summer especially you might have to wait in line for an hour or more. Alternatively, in summer go after 6pm.

Most people consider the wait worthwhile. Not that there is much to see inside: that's the whole point. The rooms in which the Franks hid are as bare as they were on the day the family was betrayed and taken to the death camp. But it is not difficult, using your imagination and powers of empathy, to put yourself in Anne's situation, awakening as a young woman, and telling her secret thoughts to the diary. Her life was extinguished; her spirit lives on.

One of four **Canal Bikes** moorings is on Prinsengracht outside the Anne Frankhuis, so if you fancy

Above: Prinsengracht houseboats
Left: Anne Frankhuis

a more light-hearted activity at this point, spend an hour pottering about on the water (but for a separate tour, see *Itinerary 7, The Canals by Canal Bike, page 42*).

Continue a few steps to **Westermarkt** and the **Westerkerk** (church: Apr–Jun Mon–Fri, July–Aug Mon–Sat, 11am–3pm; tower: Apr–Sept Mon–Sat 10am–5.30pm; church free; entrance fee for tower), a Renaissance-style church built between 1620 and 1631. The latter date marked the opening of its tower, the **Westertoren** (guided tours Jun–Sept: daily 10am–6pm; entrance fee), which is surmounted by the blue, red and gold crown of the Holy Roman Empire, a symbol bestowed by the Austrian Emperor Maximilian. Although Rembrandt was interred in the church, no trace of his tomb has ever been found. Also on Westermarkt is a sculpture of Anne Frank and the marble triangles of the **Homomonument**, dedicated to the gay and lesbian victims of persecution down the centuries.

Across the street at 33 Westermarkt, on the corner of Prinsengracht, is a lunch option, the **Kalkhoven**, a traditional old brown café with rugs on the tables and hard drinkers around the bar. Before continuing along Prinsengracht, you might want to make a short diversion, to the right, to 17 Rozengracht, to visit the **Blue Gold Fish**, an intriguingly offbeat jewellery-cum-gift shop with a style all its own.

Nine Little Streets

Continue along Prinsengracht, past the Pulitzer Hotel, to Reestraat. From here, go down to Keizersgracht, turn right and continue as far as Wolvenstraat. These connecting streets are some of the so-called Negen Straatjes (Nine Little Streets), that are noted for their many interesting and sometimes offbeat shops. At Herengracht and go right to Wijde Heisteeg, then left once again to the Singel and on to Spui. This square is quite fascinating, and is a major constituent of the next itinerary (see *Itinerary 2, The Principal Squares, page 28*). You might however want to adjourn for a coffee break here at **Café Hoppe** (18–20 Spuistraat), another traditional brown café, or at the chic **Grand-Café Luxembourg** (24 Spuistraat).

Either way, walk alongside the far bank of Singel to the **Bloemenmarkt** (Flower Market), which is one of Amsterdam's most special sites. It's like a botanical garden set along the canal, with heaps of flowers changing hands. This is probably the best – and is certainly the most atmospheric – place at which to buy cut flowers and bulbs. You are now at **Muntplein**, a busy tram intersection, and its **Munttoren** (Mint Tower). The base of the tower used to be part of the Reguliers Gate in the city wall, and in 1620 Hendrick de Keyser added the ornate, lead-covered bell tower whose bells sing out gaily every Tuesday and Friday at 12.30pm and 1pm respectively.

Turn right along Vijzelstraat to Herengracht to visit the **Kattenkabinet** (Cat Museum, 497 Herengracht; Mon–Fri 10am–2pm and 1–5pm, Sat and Sun 1–5pm;

Right: the steeple of the 17th-century Westerkerk

entrance fee). This museum is dedicated to depictions of our feline friends. Sculptures, paintings and prints show the role of the cat in art and culture through the centuries. The golden-age merchants' houses ranged along the bend in the canal at this point give rise to this neighbourhood's name: the Golden Bend.

Patrician residences

Proceed up Vijzelstraat to Keizersgracht and turn left to visit the **Museum van Loon** (672 Keizersgracht; Sept–Jun Fri–Mon 11am–5pm, July–Aug daily 11am–5pm; entrance fee). This museum gives you a glimpse behind the gables at what a patrician house – in this case a double house dating from 1672 – of the era immediately following the golden age would have looked like. Its restored period rooms are filled with richly decorated panelling, stucco work, mirrors, fireplaces, furnishings, porcelain, medallions, chandeliers, rugs, and so forth. The marble staircase, complete with intricately designed balustrade, is itself a masterpiece.

Continue across Reguliersgracht to Utrechtsestraat, a fascinating shopping street with some good restaurants, such as the Indonesian **Tempo Doeloe** at No. 75. To see another richly-decorated, 17th-century patrician canal house, head north to the junction with Herengracht and turn right to the **Willet-Holthuysen Museum** (605 Herengracht; Mon–Fri 10am–5pm, Sat and Sun 11am–5pm; entrance fee). Check out the dining salon, with a table set under the chandelier for what looks like a pretty fancy meal. A walk to the end of Herengracht is rewarded by a picturesque scene at the **River Amstel**.

Afterwards, if you want to treat yourself, return to Utrechtsestraat and dine at **Tempo Doeloe**, or one of the numerous other excellent restaurants – Dutch, ethnic, seafood, vegetarian – situated on this long street.

2. THE PRINCIPAL SQUARES *(see map, p22)*

Visit the city's main squares on this full-day tour. Highlights include tranquil Spui and the adjacent Begijnhof, glitzy Rembrandtplein, the popular Kalverstraat shopping area and the Spiegelkwartier antiques district. Finish the day at the wild and wonderful Leidseplein. This itinerary involves a lot of walking, but there are countless tempting cafés for breaks.

Start at the Dam, which can be reached by taking any of the following trams: 1, 2, 4, 5, 6, 9, 13, 16, 17, 24 and 25 from Centraal Station.

The **Dam**, which isn't a dam any more, marks the spot where the first dam was built on the River Amstel *circa* 1220, an event that led to the establishment of the city. Now it is Amsterdam's most monumental square. Before you set out from the Dam, you might want to have breakfast at the **Grand Hotel Krasnapolsky** (9 Dam). If so, it's well worth taking a turn around the ground floor of the hotel, which was opened in 1866 by a former Polish tailor; the restored Wintertuin (Winter Garden) restaurant is an extravagant example of Victorian-era aesthetics.

Beside the hotel is Amsterdam's premier department store, the **Bijenkorf** (1 Dam), to which you might want to return at a later time. Also on this side of the square is the somewhat insipid (or understated) **Nationaal Monument**, a 22-metre (72-ft) high obelisk commemorating Holland's liberation from German occupation in World War II. Cross the busy street that bisects the Dam, to the **Koninklijk Paleis** (Royal Palace; currently closed for renovations, due to be completed by Sept 2007). Constructed by Jacob van Campen between 1648 and 1655, the building served as the town hall, until Napoleon Bonaparte's younger brother Louis was appointed king of the Netherlands and took it for his palace in 1808. The Royal Palace compensates for its rather heavy-handed neo-classical exterior with an elegant interior that brims with white marble.

Church of Coronations

More interesting might be an exhibition at the neo-Gothic **Nieuwe Kerk** (New Church), the Netherlands' state church, which, when monarchs are not being crowned, is mostly used as an exhibition space and recital venue (it has two superb 16th- and 17th-century organs). Famous Dutch figures such as the 17th-century admiral Michiel de Ruyter, as well as the poet and playwright Joost van den Vondel, are buried here. The final point of interest in the Dam neighbourhood is **Madame Tussaud's** (20 Dam; mid-July–mid-Aug daily 10am–11pm, mid-Aug–mid-July daily 10am–6.30pm; entrance fee). Featured among the waxworks museum's models are Dutch personalities such as Rembrandt and Mata Hari, and a cast of international big names such as Churchill and Gandhi.

Above Left: relaxing in a café. **Left:** the Amstel skyline, illuminated at dusk
Right: the monumental Dam marks the spot where the city was founded

The Historical Museum

For some more background history, head along Kalverstraat, Amsterdam's popular pedestrians-only shopping street, to the **Amsterdams Historisch Museum** (Amsterdam Historical Museum, 92 Kalverstraat and 357 Nieuwezijds Voorburgwal; Mon–Fri 10am–5pm, Sat and Sun 11am–5pm; entrance fee). The museum takes visitors on a trip through the centuries, illustrating Amsterdam's transformation from a muddy medieval fishing village, through the expansive sea power of the golden age, to today's sophisticated metropolis. The museum is housed in a 16th-century orphanage.

If you are ready for lunch at this point, leave through the museum's Nieuwezijds Voorburgwal exit, walk a short distance to Spui then take a right into **Spuistraat**. Here, at No. 24, you will find the **Grand-Café Luxembourg**. Although in some people's opinion a tad pretentious, it serves good food – many of its dishes are specialities taken from the menus of well-regarded restaurants and cafés in the city. Alternatively you could try **Hoppe** (No 18–20), a brown café popular with students and journalists.

Browsing through Books

After lunch you should be ready for **Spui**. On one corner you will find the **Athenaeum News and Book Centre**, which has a good range of international titles. Outside is *'t Lieverdje* (Little Darling), a bronze sculpture of a boy standing with hands on hips and grinning broadly at passers-by. Every Friday there is a good second-hand book market in Spui, and a Sunday art market from March to September. Waterstone's, the British bookshop chain, has a branch on the square, although the entrance is at 152 Kalverstraat. Also superb for books is the **American Book Center**, a short way along Kalverstraat at No 185: it's open most days till 8pm, on Thursday till 10pm.

If you walk down Spui to No. 10–17, you will reach the **Begijnhof** (daily 8am–1pm; free). This beautiful, tranquil courtyard dates from 1346 and for centuries was the home of pious, unmarried Catholic laywomen – *begijns*, who lived a semi-monastic life in the service of the community. The last *begijn* died in 1970. The Begijnhof's little gabled houses, built between the 14th and 17th centuries are now the homes of elderly retired women – try not to disturb them. In spring the Begijnhof lawn's carpet of daffodils and crocuses complements the spiritual atmosphere. The Begijnhof's 17th-century Presbyterian church was originally Catholic – the *begijns* were compelled to hand it over after the triumph of Calvinism in Amsterdam. Across the lawn, **Het Houten Huys** (The Wooden House) at No. 34 dates from 1425. It is the city's oldest house and one of only two remaining wooden residences (for the other one, see *Itinerary 4, The Old Centre, page 37*).

Walk along Spui to **Rokin**, where you will see the canal-boat moorings of the Rederij P Kooij ferry company. Here too is the traditional cigar-and-pipe shop **P G C Hajenius** (Nos 92–96), whose humidors are world-renowned. Continue along Rokin to Muntplein (see *Itinerary 1, The Golden Age Canals, page 25*), then across to Reguliersbreestraat. At a later date you might want to take in a movie at the startlingly Art Deco **Tuschinski Theater** at Nos 26–28; in the meantime, take a turn around its magnificent lobby.

If you didn't have lunch, try a felafel at **Falafel Koning** in Regulierssteeg, opposite the Tuschinski – take it away to eat over a great view: the bridge over the Binnenamstel, at the point where the River Amstel runs into the city and its maze of canals. Continue into **Rembrandtplein** and check out the undistinguished statue of Rembrandt in the little garden at its centre. Busy, brassy Rembrandtplein is full of mediocre-to-average cafés, where aspiring musicians play in the evening. If you're looking for quality, try the **Café De Kroon** at No. 17, which has an excellent enclosed balcony that overlooks the square; alternatively, at No. 26–36, is **Café Schiller** – the wood-panelled bar of the Hotel Schiller. (For further options, see *Itinerary 14: Rembrandtplein, page 54*.)

Art and Antiques

Leave the square by Thorbeckeplein. If you're passing this way on a Sunday afternoon (between March and December), you will pass through the street stalls of the **Thorbeckeplein Art Market**, a sophisticated little gathering that sits somewhat incongruously beside the topless bars in this small, handsome square. Then take Herengracht, Vijzelstraat and Keizersgracht. There isn't a good way to do this by public transport, and you must at least partially retrace a section of *Itinerary 1: The Golden Age Canals (see page 23)* to Nieuwe Spiegelstraat and its extension along Spiegelgracht.

You are now in the **Spiegelkwartier** antiques district, where antiques shops are thickly clustered along the narrow street and the pretty canal. Look out for the wonderfully old-fashioned toy shop,

Above Left: gable stone at the Historical Museum. **Left:** the Hoppe brown café
Right: the Little Darling sculpture outside the Athenaeum News and Book Centre

the **Bell Tree**, at 10 Spiegelgracht. Not only do none of the toys bleep, whirr or zap, but a good many are actually made of wood.

Emerging from the antiques district into **Kleine Lijnbaansgracht**, turn right past a higgledy-piggledy row of canal houses, and a parade of restaurants, to **Leidseplein**. In the summer this district comes into its own as a centre of entertainment. In addition to the cafés, restaurants, theatres, cinemas and clubs, there is any number of diverse street performers, typically fire-eaters and buskers *(see Itinerary 13: Leidseplein, page 52)* . As you stroll around the square, soaking up the atmosphere, remember to be wary of pickpockets.

Cafés for People-watching

Leidseplein's cafés are good for people-watching. Particularly recommended is **Reijnders** at No. 6: despite being in such a touristy location, it retains elements of old-world, brown-café charm, and it has a cosy, glassed-in terrace. A good choice for afternoon tea is the Café Américain in the American Hotel (a fine example of Art Nouveau) at 97 Leidsekade.

Although by now it will be quite late in the day, there may still be people playing chess with huge plastic pieces at **Max Euweplein**, a satellite of

Leidseplein. Other attractions in the area include the **Holland Casino Amsterdam**, the mooring of Rederij Noord-Zuid (a canal-boat company) and, in and around Leidseplein, several cinemas *(see page 76)*.

Among the enormous choice of eateries in this neighbourhood, you could opt to dine at the excellent seafood restaurant, **De Oesterbar**, at 10 Leidseplein, or **Alfonso's**, a Mexican restaurant just off the square at 69 Korte Leidsedwarsstraat. After that, if you're still wide awake and suitably dressed, you may want to try your luck at the casino on Max Euweplein.

Above: the Begijnhof at Spui 10–17
Left: a fine model in the antiques district

3. THE MUSEUM QUARTER *(see map, p32)*

This itinerary focuses on the city's most important museums: the Rijksmuseum, Van Gogh Museum, and Stedelijk Museum. The route also takes in the Concertgebouw concert hall, two of the city's premier shopping streets and Vondelpark.

Start on Jan Luijkenstraat at the entrance to the Rijksmuseum, one stop east of Leidseplein by No. 2 or 5 tram.

These museums are so outstanding that, even if it happens to be a beautiful day, you might choose to sacrifice the sunshine for some high culture. Even if you know nothing of art, you will probably appreciate the offerings within their august walls.

The dominant building on Museumplein is the palatial **Rijksmuseum** (State Museum; tel: 674 7000; daily 9am–6pm; entrance fee), the most important museum in the Netherlands. However, almost all of the vast building is closed until the summer of 2008 for renovation and rebuilding. Until then, a vastly scaled-down selection of the most outstanding works is on display, under the title 'The Masterpieces', in the Museum's Philips Wing (entrance at 1 Jan Luijkenstraat). This greatly simplifies the task of getting to grips with a museum that has more than 7 million items in its collection. Even this truncated display represents one of the highlights of a visit to Amsterdam – a fact that reflects how superb this museum's collection, in particular its works from the Dutch golden age, really is.

Among other highlights on display are exquisitely detailed 17th-century dolls' houses, fully 'furnished', with tiny Delftware plates, paintings, copper plates, and precious silver, glass and porcelain objects, most of which were made by respected craftsmen. Comparable to the richly decorated cabinets of collectors, these dolls' houses were not made as playthings for children but for women of the regent and merchant classes. In addition, there is a beautiful collection of Delftware, with delightful pieces, such as a polychrome pair of pointed, high-heeled shoes and a violin, among the more familiar jugs and plates.

The Night Watch

Start with the foremost attraction, Rembrandt's *The Night Watch*. Painted in 1642, this group portrait of a colourfully attired militia company has come to represent not only Rembrandt but the entire Dutch golden age. Its iconic status might not be immediately apparent – don't be surprised if, like many visitors, you are far from overwhelmed at first sight. The militiamen themselves hated the picture and their hostile reception sent Rembrandt into a tailspin that led to bankruptcy. Yet it is a magnificent spectacle when viewed as a whole, a *tour de force* of colour, light and composition. Up

Above: a pensive cherub at the Rijksmuseum

close you can focus on the individual faces (including Rembrandt's own), which express the confidence and pride of a young nation that had liberated itself from the Spanish colonial yoke and saw an exciting new world opening up before it. Be prepared for some queuing if you want to see the work from a good vantage point.

A host of other great paintings by the Dutch masters hang on nearby walls – portraits by Frans Hals and Vermeer, landscapes by Jacob van Ruisdael, bawdy escapades by Jan Steen, and many others.

A Worthy Plaza

Leave the Rijksmuseum on Museumstraat, which cuts across **Museumplein**. Grassy areas extend uninterrupted across the square, creating a grand promenade and affording a pleasant refuge for relaxation, while making its cultural citadels easily accessible. There is a separate area for sport and play, and a bicycle path. Colourful benches and stylish lanterns have been dotted across the area. Skateboarders have their terrain on one side and boules and basketball players on the other. Across from the Rijksmuseum, the Cobra Café, pays homage to the Cobra art movement; its outdoor terrace can seat nearly 200. Just beside it a long pond freezes in winter to become an ice-skating rink. Nearby, the Van Gogh Museum and Rijks-

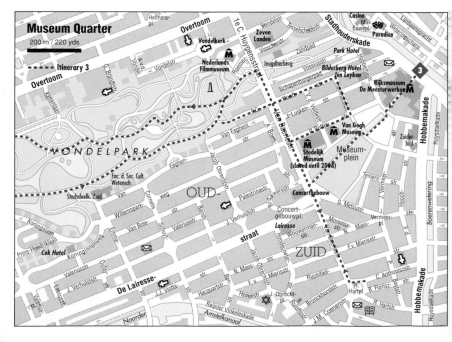

museum share a gift-shop pavilion selling posters, cards and souvenirs relating to their collections.

Walk to the end of Museumplein, to **Van Baerlestraat** and the **Concertgebouw** (Concert Building, 2–6 Concertgebouwplein). Built in 1887 by the architect A.L. van Gendt, this is one of the world's great classical music halls and the home of the Concertgebouw Orchestra. A golden lyre stands on the roof above the entrance, and the neo-classical colonnade is watched over by severe portrait busts of Beethoven, Sweelinck and Bach. Among the composers who have held court here are Brahms, Stravinsky, Strauss and Mahler. If you are here on a Wednesday around lunchtime, you may be able to listen to the orchestra rehearsing for free. Or you might want to buy tickets for an evening concert.

There is an excellent restaurant next door to the Concertgebouw, **Bodega Keyzer** (96 Van Baerlestraat), where, in a much recounted incident, a musician from the Concertgebouw Orchestra was once mistaken for a waiter. Or you could walk south along Van Baerlestraat to **De Knijp** at No. 134, which is equally good and less stuffy. For what might be the best option of all, walk a little further, to Roelof Hartplein, for lunch in the chic café-restaurant **De Wildschuut**, which has a pavement terrace, at Nos 1–3.

Modern Art

After lunch, retrace your steps along Van Baerlestraat, passing the Concertgebouw, to the **Stedelijk Museum** (Municipal Museum; 13 Paulus Potterstraat; daily 11am–5pm; tel: 573 2737; entrance fee). Unfortunately, it has completely closed the doors of its 1895 Dutch neo-Renaissance home for renovation and expansion until some time in 2008. In the meantime, most of the collection is on display on three floors of the TPG Building next to Centraal Station. The Stedelijk stretches the definition of modern art back to the mid-19th century, finishing at the end of the 20th century. It has an incredible collection of non-Dutch masters, including works by Braque, Breitner, Calder, Cézanne, Chagall, Israëls, Kandinsky, Malevich, Manet, Matisse, Monet, Oldenburg, Picasso, Renoir, Rosenquist and Warhol. The Dutch collection is outstanding, particularly the Appel collection. There are De Koonings and Mondrians here.

The last of the big three museums, the **Van Gogh Museum** (7 Paulus Potterstraat; daily 10am–6pm; tel: 570 5200; entrance fee) may be the highlight of your visit to Amsterdam. Vincent Van Gogh (1853–90) is the subject of passionate devotion throughout the world, and his paintings command astronomical prices at auction. This is particularly ironic considering the poverty and lack of recognition suffered by the artist in his short lifetime. The

Above Left: doll's house at the Rijksmuseum
Right: self-portrait at the Van Gogh Museum

museum contains some 200 Van Gogh paintings – including *The Potato Eaters* and *Sunflowers* – and 500 of his drawings, along with the artist's collection of Japanese wood carvings. The library of letters features examples of the correspondence between Vincent and his brother Theo. The museum also displays works by Toulouse-Lautrec, Gauguin and other major international artists.

Van Gogh's paintings are arranged in simple chronological order, which makes it easy to trace his development as an artist from the darkly foreboding works of his early Dutch and Belgian period, through the burgeoning of colour in Paris, to the luminous, swirling masterpieces he painted in the clear light of Provence. There is an inevitable question mark at the end of this sequence: what more would he have achieved and what recognition might he have received if he had not cut short his own life at the age of 37? Temporary exhibitions are displayed at the ellipse-shaped, partially subterranean wing designed by the Japanese architect Kisho Kurokawa.

Designer Clothes

Having had your fill of museums you might be in the mood for some shopping in Van Baerlestraat and the adjoining **Pieter Cornelisz Hooftstraat** (which is generally shortened to PC Hooftstraat, or 'the PC Hooft'), two blocks down Van Baerlestraat from the Stedelijk Museum. These are Amsterdam's two

top-rated shopping streets and it makes sense to take advantage of being in the area. Lots of smart and trendy designer-clothes outlets are located here, particularly in the PC Hooft.

On long summer evenings, you could take in the city's atmosphere by walking to the western end of PC Hooftstraat for a leisurely stroll in **Vondelpark**, named after the poet and playwright Joost van den Vondel (1587–1689). After dark this is not such a sensible option because the park becomes less attractive and less safe. The park serves as both garden and playground. In typical Dutch fashion, Vondelpark has lots of water, in the shape of long, sinuous pools around which crowds gather to sunbathe in summer. In addition to the park's usual activities – walking, cycling, jogging,

Above: shopping at the PC Hooft
Left: statue of the poet in Vondelpark

frisbee-throwing, and ice-cream guzzling – one of the most enjoyable pursuits, for the young at heart at least, is roller-blading. Rent a pair of rollerblades (and protective gear) from **Duosport Rent-a-Skate** at the Amstelveenseweg end of the park and, kitted out like an imperial stormtrooper from *Star Wars,* you can power-blade (or power-stumble) around the expanses of Vondelpark.

If it's a warm evening, dine al fresco on the terrace of Vondelpark's own **Café Vertigo**. Should something more sophisticated appeal to you, you could return to Van Baerlestraat and the **Bodega Keyzer** – be sure to order your meal from a waiter and not from the lead violin – or to **De Knijp**.

4. THE OLD CENTRE (THE WALLEN) *(see map, p36)*

Take a leisurely stroll through the infamous Rosse Buurt (Red-Light District) in daylight hours, when you can appreciate the many non-erotic attractions of this beautiful old part of Amsterdam.

Start at the Dam outside the Grand Hotel Krasnapolsky, or inside if you want breakfast at the coffee bar. Allow three hours for this itinerary.

Walk along Damrak in the direction of Centraal Station, and turn right into Beursplein. Here, in addition to the fountain and tree-shaded benches, you will find the early-20th-century **Beurs van Berlage** (1 Beursplein; Tues–Sun 11am–5pm; entrance fee). This, the old Stock Exchange, is now a museum, exhibition hall and concert venue. In its main hall you can admire the plain ironwork, narrow arcades, and Romanesque and neo-Renaissance motifs.

Take Beursstraat, then turn right onto Paternostersteeg, and continue through Wijde Kerksteeg to Oudekerksplein. (If by chance Paternostersteeg is closed, continue on to Oude Brugsteeg, turn right into Warmoesstraat, and then left into Wijde Kerksteeg for Oudekerksplein.) The foundations of the **Oude Kerk** (Old Church; Mon–Sat 11am–5pm, Sun 1–5pm; entrance fee) were laid in 1300, but the triple-naved church was not completed until 1577. A turn around the tree-shaded square gives a good impression of the Red-Light District: the venerable old church, pretty canal and gabled houses now seem rather incongruous amid the prostitutes' parlours and sex clubs.

Walk along the **Oudezijds Voorburgwal** canal, past more red-fringed rooms and a couple of good second-hand bookshops. The 17th- and 18th-century houses at Nos 101–7, 133–5, and 232 have interestingly-shaped gables. Across Damstraat, still on Oudezijds Voorburgwal, the character of the area changes to one of handsome houses and offices in the old gabled canal-side buildings. At No. 197 is **The Grand**, one of Amsterdam's

Above: cycling in Damrak

swankiest hotels, located in a 16th-century building that was once the **Prinsenhof** (Royal Inn); it's well worth entering for a look. At No. 231 the **Athenaeum Illustre**, dating from 1632, was the forerunner of the University of Amsterdam, whose campus you are now entering.

Turn left into Grimburgwal, noting the scenic junction of three canals at this point (the 17th-century house at the intersection has been dubbed the Huis aan de Drie Grachten, or House on the Three Canals). Walk to the far side of Oudezijds Achterburgwal, then right into Oudemanhuispoort, an arcade that hosts an excellent second-hand book market. Midway along the arcade, on the left, automatic doors open onto a garden courtyard. Turning left at the end of the arcade, you enter Kloveniersburgwal, passing the **Oost-Indisch Huis** (East India House), which was once the headquarters of the United East India Company and which now houses university offices. Its main entrance is on **Oude Hoogstraat**, leading back to Oudezijds Achterburgwal.

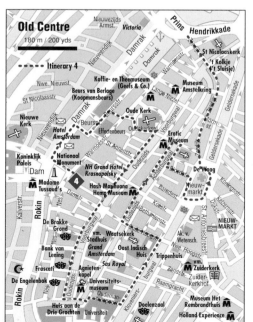

Marijuana Museum

Located on the far side of the canal are two museums that bring a touch of what you might call culture (if you're willing to stretch the term) to the Red-Light District. First up is the **Hash Marihuana Hemp Museum** (130 Oudezijds Achterburgwal; daily

Above: the Oude Kerk

11am–11pm; entrance fee). This could be described as an 'educational' experience. Amsterdam and the noxious weed are all but synonymous, and here you get the lowdown on the high. In fact, the museum is extremely well placed – this area is the centre of street drug-dealing in the city.

Then there is the **Erotic Museum** (54 Oudezijds Achterburgwal; daily 11am–1am; entrance fee), which is more about decorations of a bawdy nature. It treats its subject matter seriously, and includes 19th-century photographs showing Victorians being far from prim and proper. Above the entrance is a gable stone dating from 1685; it is decorated with a castle motif and proclaims, in the words of Martin Luther, *"God is myn burgh"* (God is my stronghold).

Cross the canal bridge and return along the canal for a short distance to Bloedstraat, then into **Nieuwmarkt**. The 14th-century **De Waag** on the square was one of the city's fortified gates. Now it is a multimedia centre with a wonderful, atmospheric restaurant, **In den Waag**. Nearby is Zeedijk, which was once a 'shooting gallery' for Amsterdam's heroin addicts. Now cleaned up, it is a fairly attractive shopping street that curves into a restaurants-and-bars zone before ending opposite Centraal Station. At No. 1 is **'t Aepjen**, a wooden house dating from 1550, one of only two such houses left in the city (for the other one, see *Itinerary 2, The Principal Squares, page 29*).

5. THE ZOO DISTRICT   *(see pull-out map)*

A half-day trip to the Botanical Gardens, Artis Zoo, and Tropical Museum.

Start at Waterlooplein, served by tram lines 9 and 14, as well as the metro to Waterlooplein station.

Either walk across Mr Visserplein to Muiderstraat, or hop on tram No. 9 or 14 for one stop. (We revisit Waterlooplein in *Itinerary 11: The Jewish Quarter, page 48*, so you may not want to linger there now.) Cross the bridge over Nieuwe Herengracht and you will see **Hortus Botanicus** (Botanical Garden, 2a Plantage Middenlaan; Feb–June and Sept–Nov: Mon–Fri 9am–5pm, Sat and Sun 10am–5pm; July–Aug: Mon–Fri 9am–9pm, Sat and Sun 10am–9pm; Dec–Jan: Mon–Fri 9am–4pm, Sat and Sun 10am–4pm; entrance fee) on your right.

Founded in 1638 as the Hortus Medicus, the Botanical Garden is one of the world's oldest. It moved to its present location in 1682. With some 250,000 flowers and 115,000 plants and trees, including 8,000 different varieties, the garden is a medley of colour and scent, and a relaxing place for a stroll. It owes much to the treasure trove of tropical plants the Dutch found in their former colonies of Indonesia, Surinam and the Antilles, and not a little of its popularity to the national infatuation with flowers – not only tulips.

Among the garden's highlights are the **Semicircle**

Right: hands-on activity at the zoo

behind the entrance – a reconstruction of part of the original layout from 1682; the **Mexico-California Desert House**; the **Palm House**, comprising one of the world's oldest collection of palm trees; and the **Tri-Climate House**, grouping tropical, subtropical and desert plants. Opened in 1993, it features a gallery that simulates the atmosphere of a jungle. You can get a snack from the **Oranjerie** (built in 1870), or you might want to check out the shop's souvenirs.

Walk or take tram Nos 9 or 14 one stop along Plantage Middenlaan to **Artis Zoo** (38–40 Plantage Kerklaan; Apr–Oct: daily 9am–6pm; Nov–Mar: daily 9am–5pm; entrance fee) – the country's oldest. Like zoos throughout the world, Artis has made a big effort to replace the cruel exploitation of animals with a facility that promotes the appreciation and preservation of the natural world's living creatures, with a particular emphasis placed on authenticity. The African Savannah, for instance, consists of a micro-plain that is home to zebras, wildebeest, ostriches and other birds. Artis, which has been open since 1838, does its best in this respect, but the animals don't have much space. Regardless, the zoo is an enormous attraction, particularly for children.

The range of animals includes tigers, leopards, elephants, camels, polar bears, gorillas, peacocks, seals and so forth. There is in addition an aviary, a reptile house, a nocturnal house, a **Planetarium** (closed Mon am) and a

Geological Museum. The zoo's garden layout and range of tree and plant species rival those of the Hortus Botanicus. The **Aquarium** is well presented, particularly the sections on the River Amazon, coral reefs, and Amsterdam's own canals, with their fish populations and urban detritus. Rest with a snack or lunch at the self-service restaurant **De Twee Cheetahs**, which features a 'kiddies' corner' and a play-island for children in front.

Continue along Plantage Middenlaan, either on foot or for two stops on the 9 or 14 tram, to the **Tropenmuseum** (Tropical Museum, 2 Linnaeusstraat; daily 10am–5pm; entrance fee). As at the Hortus Botanicus, the impetus behind the Tropenmuseum came from the Dutch colonies in the tropics. The extravagant building says a lot about the European colonial ideal. This is not to suggest that the museum is a dusty monument to vanished glory; it is a highly relevant evocation of life and environment in the tropics, with emphasis on the threats posed by burgeoning populations and ecological destruction. If you are travelling with youngsters, you could take them to the **Kindermuseum**, within the Tropenmuseum. It is designed for children, though of course adults are allowed, so long as they are in the guise of chaperones.

Once you have had your fill of flora and fauna, you can take the No. 9 or 14 tram back to Waterlooplein.

Above: a lioness extends a loud welcome to the zoo

6. THE HARBOUR *(see map, p40)*

Allow four hours for a tour of the old harbour. The itinerary covers the 'little islands' at one end and the Maritime Museum at the other, and includes a two-minute 'cruise' on the IJ ferry to Amsterdam North.

Start at Centraal Station. As you will be using public transport for part of the itinerary, make sure you have an electronic OV-chipkaart *or* strippenkaart *(strip ticket), or buy one from the bus driver* (see Practical Information: Getting Around, page 83).

It's well worth taking the time to have a good look at **Centraal Station**. Constructed on an artificial island in the IJ channel, the station opened in 1895 and was heartily disliked at the time. Today the station is a tourist attraction in its own right, partly for its extravagant architecture and partly for the lively atmosphere that surrounds it. Street musicians, particularly traditional barrel-organ grinders, for some reason, line up to perform here. Twelve of the city's 17 tram routes begin and end their journeys at Centraal Station, as do three of the four metro lines, and a number of bus routes. The station is undergoing redevelopment and expansion, to make way for a new metro station and improve its facilities for water-transport on the IJ channel.

Two VVV (local tourism) centres – one inside and the other outside the station – dispense information and book hotel rooms for tourists. If you haven't had breakfast or you want a coffee, the **1e Klas** buffet on platform one is excellent.

There are enough bicycles chained up in this area to constitute an obstacle to navigation. The Museumboot (Museum Boat) also stops at the station. A note of warning – beware of pickpockets in this area.

Now it is time to hit the water. For a good view of Amsterdam harbour, take one or both

Above: Centraal Station
Right: old-time barrel organ

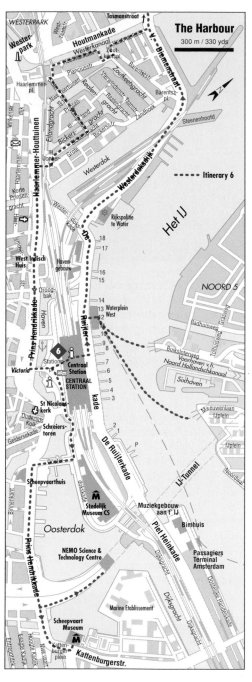

The Harbour
300 m / 330 yds

----- Itinerary 6

of the ferries that cross the IJ channel from a pier at the rear of Centraal Station. Unusually for Amsterdam, the shortest ferry trips are free. The **Buiksloterwegveer** is a covered landing craft that crosses the channel in two minutes, while the **Adelaarswegveer** looks more like a real boat, and takes all of five minutes for its crossing to a point further east. Both vessels will transport your bicycle (or other two-wheeled vehicles).

River Traffic

On the way across the busy channel you will probably intersect the wakes of canal boats and pleasure boats, and perhaps a visiting warship or an ocean-going cruise liner. Watch out for the Royal Dutch Shell office tower on the north bank – its windows are laced with gold dust and sparkle in the sunlight.

There is not a great deal to see in Amsterdam North, which is mostly a modern residential area, and you probably won't want to spend much time on the north bank. Ferries come and go every few minutes, so you should not have very long to wait before returning to Centraal Station.

Take the No, 35 bus from the stop outside Centraal Station on De Ruijterkade (beside the Holland International canal-boat jetty) to Tasmanstraat. Or you might decide to walk there; the road has a good view of the harbour. There are no famous monuments or tourist attractions in this neighbourhood – the point is to experience the old harbour's ambience. On the left side of Tasmanstraat is a cramped area – full of characterful warehouses, docks, small boatyards and other harbour installations – that is being converted into residences.

Take a stroll down Houtmankade, passing the children's playground on Zoutkeetsplein, until you reach the end of Houtmankade, then turn left onto Schiemanstraat and Sloterdijkstraat. Walk across the narrow bridge over Prinseneilandsgracht, to Galgenstraat and Kleine Bickersstraat. Then, by way of Bickersstraat and Jonkerplein, walk under the railway bridge to the bus stop on Haarlemmer Houttuinen.

Having acquainted yourself with this part of the harbour, take the No. 22 bus back to Centraal Station. You can either get out and walk to Kattenburgerplein, or continue there on the No. 22 (a break at Centraal Station gives you another opportunity to sample the delights served up by the station buffet). Note that just east of the station, at 5 Oosterdokskade, is the temporary (until 2008) home of the Stedelijk Museum *(see Itinerary 3, The Museum Quarter, page 33)*.

Once at Kattenburgerplein, cross to the **Scheepvaart Museum** (Maritime Museum, 1 Kattenburgerplein; Oct–May: Tues–Sun 10am–5pm; June–Sept: Mon–Sun 10am–5pm; entrance fee). Housed in the former Amsterdam Admiralty building, dating from 1656, the museum documents and celebrates Holland's sea-faring history, with a pronounced emphasis on the 17th century, when the country was one of the world's great sea powers.

A full-scale replica of the 17th-century Dutch East Indiaman, the *Amsterdam*, is moored to a jetty outside the museum. It presents a fantastic sight, a squat yet elegant mountain of timber surmounted by three tall masts and threaded with a tracery of rigging. Breezes from the nearby shipping channel roil the water and set the *Amsterdam* swaying gently at her moorings. Below decks, in the crew's quarters and cargo hold, the vessel's timbers creak and groan alarmingly, creating an evocative impression of conditions on such a craft when rounding the Cape of Good Hope and facing the full force of a storm in the Indian Ocean.

Science and Technology

Follow the waterfront around Kattenburgerplein, past a sculpture of Amphitrite, to the long stairway that leads up to the wonderful **NEMO Science and Technology Centre** (2 Oosterdok; July–Aug: daily 10am–5pm; Sept–June: Tues–Sun 10am–5pm; entrance fee),. Like its many interactive exhibits, the centre's futuristic architecture reflects the high-tech experience of life in the 21st century. All exhibits at this child-friendly place have explanation in English and there are guided tours.

Top: mooring a boat at the harbour
Right: at the Maritime Museum

7. THE CANALS BY CANAL BIKE   *(see pull-out map)*

Take a mini-cruise, riding a water-bike along the canals.

Start at the canal-bike mooring on Prinsengracht, next to the Anne Frankhuis. You can start at any of Canal Bike's four moorings (the other three are at Leidseplein, Keizersgracht/Leidsestraat and the Rijksmuseum) and return the bike to any of them. Allow for two or three hours.

Amsterdammers look down their noses at water-bikes; tourists seem to love them. Amsterdam is best seen from the water, and as captain of a two- or four-person water bike you can navigate your way through the canal network. For information, contact **Canal Bike** (tel: 020-626 5574).

You will be told the rules when you hire a water-bike: you cannot sail on the IJ channel or the River Amstel, and there may be other places that are out of bounds. You can buy a brochure and map that outline five routes. The canals

can get busy, so watch out for potential problems, particularly when passing under bridges. In bad weather, the bikes, which are safe and unsinkable, can be fitted with rainshields.

Side-canals

Pedal southwards along Prinsengracht, past Lauriergracht, Looiersgracht and then Passeerdersgracht. Take the opportunity to turn into one or more of these side canals, which are quiet but interesting. At Leidsegracht, you can turn off, but it's better to plough straight ahead, under Leidsestraat, until you reach the pretty **Spiegelgracht**, where you should turn right. Continue to the end then turn left under the bridge into Lijnbaansgracht.

Turn right after the **Mankind** café at the first corner on the right to a short, dark and dank canal alongside Weteringstraat. Keep going under the Weteringspoort Bridge and re-emerge with the Rijksmuseum ahead. Turn right into Singelgracht, where you can leave your bike at the mooring, if you want to. If you continue the trip, you'll find a greener canalside, with overhanging trees in the gardens of villas that are now mostly offices.

You're entering busier waters now, as you pass the Lido and its waterfront café terrace, then Leidseplein and the Art Nouveau **American Hotel**, opposite which is another mooring where you can deposit the bike. Otherwise, to complete the circuit, pass the **Bellevue Theater** and the **De la Mar Theater** and turn right into Leidsegracht, which brings you back to Prinsengracht and a straight run back to Westermarkt.

Above: local people don't like them, but water-bikes are popular with visitors

8. AMSTERDAM BY TRAM   *(see pull-out map)*

Riding Amsterdam's trams is fun, fast and convenient. This express-tram itinerary passes many of the city's highlights, and the new business and residential districts on the outskirts. It takes about two hours.

Start from Centraal Station. Take the blue tram No. 5 from the stop to your left as you face the station. Buy an electronic OV-chipkaart *or a* strippenkaart *(strip ticket) from the on-board ticket machine or use one you bought previously. This itinerary covers three zones, so insert the fourth available strip in one of the on-board validation machines.*

As the tram emerges from Centraal Station, keep an eye open for the 1629 brown café **De Karpershoek** to your right on the corner of Martelaars-gracht. The tram rolls along Nieuwezijds Voorburgwal and stops at a building with pear-shaped towers that was formerly the main Post Office and is now the **Magna Plaza** shopping centre. To your left is the rear of the **Royal Palace**. Further ahead, towards Spui, the tram passes the **Amsterdams Historisch Museum** on your left.

Note the excellent Indonesian restaurant **Kantjil de Tijger** beside the tram stop at Spui. You swing around Koningsplein and into **Leidsestraat**, which is a notable shopping street. The tram stops on the bridges across **Keizersgracht** and **Prinsengracht**, giving passengers a fine view along the canals. Leidseplein is one of the places at which you might get off, for a stroll around Amsterdam's most happening square. The **Stadsschouwburg** (City Theatre) is the red-brick building beside the stop, and the Art Nouveau **American Hotel** the multi-turreted extravaganza that follows it.

As the tram turns hard left onto Stadhouderskade, get ready for some rapid-fire switches of attention from right to left and back again. To your left is the **Holland Casino Amsterdam**, then to your right the entrance to **Vondelpark**. You veer into Hobbemastraat, with the illustrious **Pieter Cornelisz Hooftstraat** shopping thoroughfare and **Coster Diamonds** to your right, and the **Rijksmuseum** to your left, then into Paulus Potterstraat, where, in quick succession out of the left-side window, you will notice the

Van Gogh Museum and the **Stedelijk Museum** (closed here until 2008) of modern-art. Now the tram turns left into Van Baerlestraat, where the **Concertgebouw** lies to your right and the long vista of Museumplein to your left.

Into the Suburbs

Further along, you turn right on a road leading to Beethovenstraat, from which point there are fewer landmarks to see and you can relax. Now the tram, liberated from the city centre's constricted streets, picks up the pace. The view is one of apartment blocks, at least until you reach the big, blue-glass-fronted **World Trade Centre Amsterdam**, known locally as the Blauwe Engel (Blue Angel). Other modern office towers line the adjacent motorway until the tram turns left into Buitenveldertselaan, with the **Vrije Universiteit** (Free University) to your right – look out for the giant bicycle parking lot in front of the university.

The tram rushes ever faster through the dormitory suburbs of Buitenveldert and Amstelveen, until it takes a hard right off Beneluxbaan and stops a few seconds later at the terminus beside the **Amstelveen Shopping Centre**. This is a good place for out-of-town shopping although, predictably, it lacks the character of the city centre. If you're feeling peckish, walk just a few metres to the **Vroom & Dreesmann** department store. V&D has a justifiably popular sandwich counter, at which you can order your choice of fillings before watching the sandwich being prepared on fresh-baked bread in front of you.

Return Journey

You might, for the sake of variety, decide to return by a different route, in which case walk to the stop on Beneluxbaan. The imposing white building you pass on the way is another modern art centre – the **Cobra Museum** (1–3 Sandebergplein; Tues–Sun 11am–5pm), dedicated to the art movement after which it is named. Take the metro in the direction of Centraal Station. You retrace the previous route as far as the World Trade Centre before passing the enormous **rai Congresgebouw** (Congress Centre) to your left and, by way of any number of tortuous twists and turns and subterranean tunnels, join the metro line inbound to the city centre. Beyond **Amstel Station**, the line runs underground, taking you quickly back to Centraal Station.

9. BY BICYCLE ALONG THE RIVER AMSTEL
(see pull-out map)

Cycle along a fairly quiet riverside route and emerge in the countryside on the way to the pretty village of Ouderkerk aan de Amstel. Allow four or five hours.

Start at Waterlooplein, which is served by tram lines 9 and 14 and the metro.

The best place from which to rent a bicycle in this district is **Mac Bike** (2 Mr Visserplein, tel: 020-620 0985), off the north side of Waterlooplein. *(For details on Waterlooplein see Itinerary 11, The Jewish Quarter, page 48.)* Cycle to the right (east) bank of the **River Amstel**, passing but not crossing the **Blauwbrug** (Blue Bridge) connecting Waterlooplein and Amstelstraat. Houseboats are moored along the river here and the scene on the water is likely to be quite busy. You'll also pass the neo-classical Amstelhof, a nursing home dating from 1681 and currently being prepared to accommodate changing elements from the collection of St Petersburg's State Hermitage Museum, under the title **Hermitage Amsterdam** (tel: 530 8755; open daily 10am–5pm; entrance fee). The first section opened in 2004 in the Neerlandia Building, an annexe of the Amstelhof, with entrance at 14 Nieuwe Herengracht.

Continue to the **Magere Brug**, the 'Skinny Bridge' over the Amstel, an 18th-century replacement for the original 17th-century bridge. Note the fine local eatery **De Magere Brug** (81 Amstel), whose guest book was signed by the Scottish pop singer Rod Stewart, with the commendation, 'Nice ham 'n' eggs'.

Cross to the left bank and continue south. You should be able to see the **Theater Carré**, on the other side of the water. Continue over the tram lines on Sarphatistraat. Make a detour around a break in the riverside road, over busy Stadhouderskade and back to the river at **Amsteldijk**.

Keep pedalling south until you reach the **Berlage Brug**, where the traffic becomes busier. At **Martin Luther King Park** most of the traffic swings away on President Kennedylaan, leaving you still on the

Amsteldijk, which is now almost rural, with houseboats in place of cottages. The thundering noise you begin to hear up ahead might sound like a Niagara-sized waterfall, but is actually the traffic on the A10 Ringweg Zuid bridge.

You're in the countryside now, passing Amstel Park and a pretty, if rather kitsch, scene of a windmill and a statue of Rembrandt. Beyond this is a great café/restaurant, **Het Kalfje**, with an attracitve riverside terrace on the other side of the road. (There used to be a road sign that read, 'Caution: Waiter Crossing'.)

The river is scenic and tranquil as you pass villas and cottages en route to **Ouderkerk aan de Amstel**. This village has plenty of restaurants and cafés with waterside terraces, and is good for exploring by bike. If you want to eat here, you can do no better than the **Paardenburg** (5 Strandvlietlaan).

Left: technology comes alive over the Amstel
Right: three on a bike

Return Ride

Switch to the right bank to return. This road – Ouderkerkerdijk – passes through some delightful hamlets; look out for another windmill. Recross the river at the **Utrechtse Brug**, which marks your return to the urban scene. Take Amsteldijk to the Berlage Brug. At this point you can either recross and cycle to **Amstel Station**, from where you and your bike can board a metro to Waterlooplein, or cycle back along whichever bank takes your fancy.

10. THE JORDAAN   *(see map, p47)*

This working-class district has been subject to gentrification, but plenty of its original charm remains. Allow two hours for this afternoon stroll.

Start this itinerary beside the Noorderkerk at Noordermarkt. To get there from Centraal Station, you can either take the Opstapper minibus or walk along Prins Hendrikkade to Haarlemmer Houttuinen and Prinsengracht.

The great golden-age canals of 17th-century Amsterdam were intended to serve the homes of the nobility and wealthy merchants; artisans and labourers were consigned to the **Jordaan** – a grid of streets and narrow canals cut east–west. The Jordaan's name may derive from the French *jardin* (garden), possibly in reference to the market gardens maintained by the original inhabitants. For a description of the Noordermarkt and Noorderkerk (North Church), see *Itinerary 1: The Golden Age Canals, page 23.*

Walk to **Brouwersgracht** (the Brewers' Canal), with its houseboats and rows of old warehouses, now converted into chic apartments. If you want a coffee or beer, try the traditional brown café **'t Papeneiland** (2 Prinsengracht) on the corner. Otherwise turn left on Brouwersgracht, past a sculpture of the writer Theo Thijssen (1879–1943).

Go as far as Palmgracht, onto which you should turn left. Notice the sculpted turnip on the gable at No. 28, a house dating from 1648. The house is named De Raep (The Turnip), after its owner. Then turn left into Palm Dwarsstraat and continue walking along Tweede Goudsbloemdwarsstraat as far as Lindengracht, which was once a canal. On Saturday, a street market spreads its stalls along this road.

True Amsterdammers

Off Lindengracht you will find **Karthuizerplantsoen**, a square that honours a now-vanished Carthusian monastery. Adjacent Karthuizersstraat has a row of neck-gabled houses (Nos 11, 13, 15, 17 and 19), dating from 1737 and named after the four seasons: De Lente, De Zomer, De Herfst, and De Winter (spring, summer, autumn, winter). The **Huys-Zitten-Weduwe-Hofje** at Nos 61–191 has a tree-shaded courtyard with a double garden. The small

ve: walking the dogs in one of the many open spaces in and around the city

houses here, now largely students' quarters, were once the homes of poor widows. Turn into Tichelstraat, from which you can see the Westerkerk tower in the distance: in much the same way that true London Cockneys must be born within the sound of Bow bells, so Jordaanees must be born within earshot of the Westerkerk bells. Cross Westerstraat, which was also formerly a canal.

Café Stop

Tweede Anjeliersdwarsstraat, on which you should now find yourself, has an excellent, brown-café-style restaurant, **De Eettuin**, at No. 10. (There are lots of cafés and small boutiques in this neighbourhood.) Drop down a block to Eerste Tuindwarsstraat and Eerste Egelantiersdwarsstraat. On the way, between Tuinstraat and Egelantiersstraat, a passage on the right leads to the **Claes Claesz Hofje**: two attractive little courtyards surrounded by tiny flats.

Turn right on Egelantiersgracht, a quiet canal that is lined with some interesting 17th- and 18th-century houses. On this corner, the hardware store at Nos 2–6, which dates from 1927, is an example of architecture of the Amsterdam School. Beside it is another excellent old brown café, **'t Smalle,** with a canal side terrace. There are three beautiful bell gables at Nos 61–65, one of which features a carved falcon. Don't miss the **Andrieshofje** at Nos 107–45, where a corridor lined with blue-and-white tiles leads into an attractive flower-bedecked courtyard.

Now retrace your steps, right into Tweede Leliedwarsstraat, and then continue to Bloemgracht – one of the most impressive of Jordaan's canals. From here you can see the Westerkerk tower off to your left high above the rooftops. Note the carved gablestones at Nos 77–81; these date back to 1642 and represent a townsman, a countryman and a seaman.

To end your afternoon, walk back towards **Prinsengracht,** turn right, and cross the bridge over the canal, to where the Anne Frankhuis and the nearby Westerkerk stand.

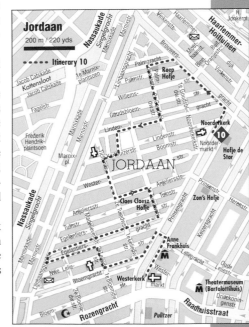

Above: at 't Papeneiland brown café

11. THE JEWISH QUARTER
(see map right)

Most of the thriving community of the Jodenbuurt (Jewish Quarter) was wiped out in the Holocaust, but a number of Jewish elements remain in this distinctive part of the city. Allow for a four-hour walk.

Start at Waterlooplein, served by tram lines 9 and 14, and by metro.

This itinerary begins with the multifarious offerings of the **flea market** (Mon–Sat 10am–4pm) on the west and north sides of **Waterlooplein**. In the 19th century the Dutch author Multatuli wrote of the market: 'There were headless nails, toothless saws, bladeless chisels, locks without springs, keys without locks, hooks without eyes and eyes without hooks, buckles without prongs…' You may well find that little has changed, except that there are many genuine bargains among the mess and the market is more business-orientated, with less ambience, than formerly.

'Stop the Stopera'

Just as construction of the metro line under your feet was the cause of rioting in the 1970s, so in the 1980s the nascent 'Stopera' building brought protesters and water cannon back onto the streets. The name was derived from the **Stadhuis** (Town Hall) and the new **Opera** (better known as the **Muziektheater**) that were built together on the square. 'Stop the Stopera' was the popular, but ultimately ineffectual, slogan; both institutions are now firmly established, and the Muziektheater is a star in the city's cultural firmament.

Cross the square and walk through the short Turfsteeg alley to the **Joods Historisch Museum** (Jewish Historical Museum, 2–4 Jonas Daniël Meyerplein; daily 11am–5pm; entrance fee) in the former Ashkenazi Synagogue, restored following its destruction in World War II. The museum has artefacts pertaining to the 400-year history and culture of Holland's Jewish community. The displays feature paintings, books, and religious and household objects.

Cross over Mr Visserplein to the historic **Portuguese Synagogue** (3 Mr Visserplein; Apr–Oct: Sun–Fri 10am–6pm; Nov–Mar: Sun–Thur 10am–6pm, Fri 10am–3pm), dating from 1665. It was built by Sephardic Jews fleeing the latest bout of religious persecution in Spain and Portugal. Outside the

Above: flea-market mannequin
Right: spring blooms in Amsterdam

synagogue, the Dockworker Monument honours Amsterdam workers – not just dockers – who went on strike in February 1941 to protest against the Nazis' deportation of the city's Jews. The strike was savagely suppressed.

Take Weesperstraat across the bridge over the Nieuwe Herengracht to the garden, on the right side of the road. Here another statue relating to the Holocaust, a 1950 monument in the form of an altar, is dedicated to the Dutch people who protected and hid Jews during the war. Retrace your steps and recross Mr Visserplein, past the neoclassical **Mozes en Aäronkerk** on the corner of Waterlooplein. This Roman Catholic church was built on a spot where, in the 16th century, Catholics worshipped in secret to avoid problems with the Calvinist authorities. At 17 Waterlooplein, **Holland Experience** (daily 11am–7pm; entrance fee) presents a multimedia film show to demonstrate some of the country's most pertinent features. These include a simulation of what would happen if the sea dykes collapsed, complete with flowing water.

Continue to Jodenbreestraat and Sint-Antoniesbreestraat, which was once the centre of Jewish life in the city and is now partly redeveloped. You should visit the **Museum Het Rembrandthuis** (Rembrandt House Museum, 4–6 Jodenbreestraat; Mon–Sat 10am–5pm, Sun 1–5pm), where the artist lived and worked until his bankruptcy in 1658. The house has been restored as closely as possible to how it looked at that time.

Return to Waterlooplein and pass the Stadhuis to the black-marble **Jewish Resistance Fighters' Memorial** on the corner of the square. Finish at the stylish **Grand Café Dantzig aan de Amstel** next to the memorial.

12. AMSTERDAMSE BOS *(see pullout map)*

For a breath of fresh air outside the confines of the city, visit the large wooded park on the southern outskirt, where many Amsterdammers go to escape the stresses of city life. This is the countryside on the city's doorstep. Take a picnic. Allow at least four hours.

From Centraal Station take the No. 16 tram to Amstelveenseweg.

If your stay in Amsterdam is long enough to accommodate a slightly out-of-town excursion, **Amsterdamse Bos** (Amsterdam Wood) makes for a nice day out. In the summer you can reach the park by old-style tram from Haarlemmermeerstation just north of the Olympic Stadium. This service is courtesy of the Electric Tramline Museum, whose collection of antique trams has

been drawn from various European countries. Otherwise, from the bus stop on Stadionplein, take any bus going out of town for several stops along Amstelveenseweg to the entrance to the Amsterdamse Bos. Or you could walk there under the viaduct of the A10 Ring Road and past the **Vrij Universiteit Hospital**, but you might want to save your time and shoe leather for the park.

Although it might seem entirely natural, the Amsterdamse Bos, like so much of the Netherlands, is artificial. It was created in the 1930s, transforming what had been an expanse of open polders to the south of the city into a public park, not least to provide employment – this was the era of the Great Depression. All the work was completed by men and horses.

Today the 800-ha (2,000-acre) park is an important ecological site. It serves as the home to numerous species of birds, insects and small animals. Moreover, it incorporates almost 160km (100 miles) of footpaths, and some 48km (30 miles) of bicycle paths. This means that even on the busiest summer day, there is plenty of scope to avoid the crowds.

Café Bosrand beside the entrance is a reasonable place for lunch. Take Koenenkade into the park. At the Bosbaan take a right over the canal bridge, then onto another bridge over a shallow inlet to the edge of **Nieuwe Meer**, a surprisingly tranquil lake on the edge of the busy ring road and Schiphol Airport.

Messing about in Boats

Follow the path to the **Roeibaan**, a 2-km (almost 1 mile) rowing course. At the eastern end of this long, straight stretch of water is a cluster of rowing stations and pavilions, where on most days you will see rowing enthusiasts setting up their craft. At this end of the rowing course is the **Grand-Café De Bosbaan**, which has a fine terrace overlooking the water. Near the café, at the park's Bezoekerscentrum (Visitor Centre; open daily noon–5pm), you can trace the park's history and learn about the wildlife that can be found here. And just across the way is a stall where you can hire bicycles to tour the park.

Above: picnic in the Amsterdamse Bos.

Follow the Roeibaan to its western end (which is the start of the rowing course). En route you will probably pass a long line of anglers. Just beyond here is a self-service restaurant, **Boerderij Meerzicht**, which is probably the best of the park's eateries, especially for light fare such as pancakes.

From here, if you have enough time, you can choose to explore the great expanse of the Amsterdamse Bos proper, stretching southward to open moors where a herd of Scottish Highland cattle grazes. Alternatively, retrace your steps past the western end of the rowing course and take the tree-lined path to the big **Grote Vijver** pond and the nearby, 1,500-seat **Openluchttheater** (Open-air Theatre), where there are often performances on summer evenings. You can hire boats and paddle around the pond or simply enjoy the scenery and fresh air. Don't forget you have to walk the length of the Roeibaan again to reach the exit and catch the bus back to the centre.

13. LEIDSEPLEIN *(see pullout map)*

The Leidseplein area constitutes one of the centres of the city's nightlife, with many of its most popular bars, restaurants and nightclubs all in close proximity. The area never really closes, so if you have the energy you can dance the night away and still be up to greet the dawn. This tour highlights some of the most interesting possibilities.

Start at Leidseplein, reached by trams 1, 2, 5 and 6 from Centraal Station.

When planning a night out on **Leidseplein**, it can be difficult knowing where to start. A clockwise circuit will help to familiarise you with its attractions. One of the foremost of these, at No. 15, is the **Bulldog Palace**. This gruff and bristly standard-bearer of the genre is one of the 'smoking coffee shops' for which Amsterdam is famous. 'Smoking' refers to marijuana and hashish, both of which, though technically illegal have been officially 'tolerated' in the Netherlands for years. Numerous foreign pot smokers make their way to Amsterdam specifically to puff their way through as much of these soft drugs as they can. In the Bulldog, as in most of these places, it'll mostly be tourists you'll be peering at through the fog of bitter-smelling smoke.

From Cinemas to the Casino

An extension of Leidseplein is a smaller square, **Kleine Gartmanplantsoen**, in which, at Nos 13–25, you will find the seven-screen **City** complex. These tend to show the latest releases from Hollywood with Dutch subtitles.

Across the street is one of the best café-restaurants in the square – **De Balie** (10 Kleine Gartmanplantsoen), a chic place that serves great snacks on the ground floor and has a good restaurant upstairs. Left of the Balie as you face it is a passage leading to **Max Euweplein**, the home of **Holland Casino Amsterdam**, the city's only legally recognised casino (to gain entry you must

Right: *Maître d'* at the Café Américain on Leidsestraat *(see pages 52 and 69)*

be properly dressed and show your passport). Alternatively, the **Comedy Club** (No. 29) is a bar that often features fast-paced humour in English.

If seeing and being seen is more your thing, return to Leidseplein. Across Leidsestraat is the Art Nouveau **American Hotel**, whose stylish **Bar Américain** is a showcase for Amsterdam's beautiful people. For people-watching on the square, the hotel's street-level **Night Watch** bar is a good bet even though it is a bit removed from the action. A short way along Marnixstraat from here is the four-screen Bellevue-Calypso cinema complex (Nos 400–2).

Across Marnixstraat, back at Leidseplein, the **Stadsschouwburg** (City Theatre) at No. 26 stages most of its dramatic productions in Dutch, but it does sometimes feature visiting musicals from London's West End and New York's Broadway, as well as dance performances. Also located in Leidseplein, at No. 12, is the excellent **Boom Chicago Theater**, which specialises in improvisational comedy, much of it in English, that can be enjoyed over dinner.

Blast from the Past

For a less formal, more alternative experience, take Lijnbaansgracht next to the theatre to **Melkweg** (Milky Way, No. 234). The heyday of this entertainment mecca was 30 years ago, at the height of the hippie era. But far from fading into acide-fuelled oblivion, the Melkweg has constantly reinvented its multimedia image – it has a restaurant, coffee shop, bar, art centre, dance theatre, disco, cinema and concert hall among its facilities.

Adjacent to the Stadsschouwburg and the Boom Chicago is a mass of busy cafés, the terraces of which extend into the square in sunny – and not-so-sunny – weather. Though they are all very much alike, the brown-café-style **Reijnders** at No 6 is particularly recommended.

A short distance further along the street, at No. 10, **De Oesterbar** is a very popular seafood restaurant, while **Akbar** at 15 Korte Leidsedwarsstraat is a fairly reliable Indian option. On the other side of the square, on the con-

tinuation of Korte Leidsedwarsstraat, you will find **The Rookies**, at Nos 145–47, is a popular smoking coffee shop comparable to The Bulldog but of a more mellow disposition.

In a slightly wider zone around Leidseplein, embedded in a blur of cafés, restaurants and neon, are all manner of opportunities to sample live music. If you are a jazz aficionado, the music is generally of a high standard at the **Alto Jazz Café** (115 Korte Leidsedwarsstraat). You will find blues aplenty at **Bourbon Street** (6 Leidsekruisstraat); and new styles of music at **Paradiso** (6–8 Weteringschans). If you're willing to take a tram for a couple of stops along Lijnbaansgracht, one of the city's best blues venues, **Maloe Melo**, is within range at No. 63 Lijnbaansgracht.

Left: to your health

14. REMBRANDTPLEIN *(see pullout map)*

Rembrandtplein has a more downmarket reputation than Leidseplein, yet it often seems even more intent on having fun.

Start at Muntplein on the corner of Reguliersbreestraat, which can be reached by Nos 4, 9, 14, 16, 24 and 25 trams.

Take particular care when crossing busy Muntplein to Reguliersbreestraat not to get hit by a tram. There are a couple of peep-show joints on this street, but in a field not renowned for its sophistication these venues are on the tacky side. More interesting is the six-screen **Tuschinski Theater Cinema** (26–28 Reguliersbreestraat), housed in an Art Deco masterpiece.

Go left on Halve Maansteeg alley to the Amstel. If Dutch cabaret-theatre appeals, the **Kleine Komedie** (56–58 Amstel) is a great venue for what is a lively and inventive satirical scene in Holland. A few doors further along on Amstel is **Mulligan's Irish Music Bar** (No. 100) where the music and the *craic* are so authentic you could be downing a pint of Guinness in Dublin. Also along this stretch of the riverside Amstel is an enclave of gay bars and clubs, not all of them exactly salubrious. The best is the traditional **Amstel Taveerne** (No. 54), which still indulges in old-fashioned Dutch singalongs.

If the Gaelic experience doesn't appeal, three local options might. The young at heart should keep going to No. 178, where they will find the **Willems Club** dance-bar. Around the corner from here, at 3 Wagenstraat, is **Sinners in Heaven**, a trendy dance-club. At the other end of the spectrum is the **Muziektheater**, the city's premier venue for ballet and opera, at 22 Waterlooplein (make your way to the end of Amstel and glance across the river; you can't easily miss a building that's been likened by Amsterdammers to a set of false teeth). Those who appreciate the opportunity to walk, or rather dance, on the wild side should turn back along Amstelstraat to No. 24 and **iT**. Though an ostentatiously gay dance-club, it also stages mixed nights.

Above: Rembrandtplein has any number of restaurants and cafés with terraces

Music Spectrum

Rembrandtplein is a brash and brassy square that really comes into its own at night when it is awash with neon. At No. 46 there's a British-style pub, the Old Bell which, although somewhat dreary, at least allows for a restful break. **Café Schiller** (No. 36) is an island of chic. Live music to drink to, and dance to if you can find space, is offered by **Shorts of London**, but you won't win points for being hip. At the smart **Café De Kroon** opposite (No. 17) drinking and dining is seriously trendy; at **Zilver** (No. 19), jazz is on offer. For some local flavour there are other cafés in the square where locals and out-of-town Dutch like to assemble for a knees-up to schmaltzy songs.

Turn into Thorbeckeplein where, tucked in among numerous topless bars and 'exotic' floorshows, is a hot-wired jazz venue, the **Heeren van Aemstel** (No. 5). For Caribbean dancing and salsa parties at **Club Margaritas** (Nos 100–14), take Reguliersdwarsstraat at the corner of Rembrandtplein and Thorbeckeplein.

If you have enough stamina left and there's still time before dawn, you can merge this nightlife itinerary with the previous, Leidseplein itinerary. Continue across Vijzelstraat to Leidsestraat at the end of Reguliersdwarsstraat to take in music venues such as **Duivel** (No. 87), **Madeliefje** (No. 74) for salsa, and **Korte Golf** (No. 41) on the way.

15. RED-LIGHT DISTRICT *(see pullout map)*

This is a place many visitors want to see even if they don't want to participate. One of the best times to come is dusk, when the red lights glow with Japanese-lantern charm on the inky surface of the canals and business gets into full swing. Allow from one hour to all night.

Start at the Dam outside the Grand Hotel Krasnapolsky. There is no problem about women going around in groups of two or more but a single female might be subject to misrepresentation.

'Cover me. I'm going in,' reads a folksy advert for condoms, a much-requested item of apparel in the Red-Light District. So, hitch your money-

belt a notch tighter and keep your hands where everybody can see them. We're going in.

Lots of visitors do this kind of itinerary out of curiosity or just for fun. You don't need to worry overly about crime as long as you stick to the busier streets. You can banter with the girls in the windows (most of them accept their role as tourist attractions), but it is inadvisable to try and snap pictures of them unless you are dressed for swimming in the canal.

Take Damstraat at the side of the Krasnapolsky to the canal-side on Oudezijds Voorburgwal, turn left, and you're there. This is a fairly easy introductory step,

as business behind the red-fringed windows doesn't really start to get brisk until you reach the area around the **Oude Kerk** (Old Church, covered in *Itinerary 4, The Old Centre, page 35*). Turn left into Oudekerksplein, and then left again into Sint-Annendwarsstraat. Sexy Land (No 48), in the shadow of the venerable church, is more or less typical of the fare on offer all over, with private cabins and a live show.

For an even closer experience of the often suffocating atmosphere of the district, stroll down the short Trompetersteeg from Sint-Annendwarsstraat back to Oudezijds Voorburgwal. You have literally to squeeze past the women in the doorways of this constricted alleyway, giving them the ideal opportunity for a form of one-to-one marketing.

Heart of the Area

Continue past the Oude Kerk and go right across the bridge. Turn right onto **Oudezijds Voorburgwal**, which is the heart of the surprisingly small red-light district. You might want to saunter into some of the street's many bookshops, video libraries or specialised appliances shops crammed around here. If you do you will encounter knowledgeable specialists in diverse areas of human relationships.

The Sex Palace (No. 84) shows a less-than-admirable determination to get to the bottom of its subject matter. Casa Rosso (Nos 106–8) proudly considers itself the market leader in live shows. To bolster its cultural credentials it translates this description into several languages (in French, for example, the entertainment on offer sounds like a riverside village near Paris: *Baiser sur scène*).

You will no doubt find a good deal to entertain, horrify, depress or bore you, depending on your slant. My favourite address is the **Amusement Centre** (1 Molensteeg). I always leave thoroughly amused. Try it and see.

Left: where there are red lights in the windows, the entertainment is for adults
Above: just one out of a huge number of different options

excursions

Excursions

1. HAARLEM AND ZANDVOORT   *(see map p58)*

Haarlem can justifiably claim to share many of Amsterdam's advantages – fascinating history, pleasing atmosphere, 17th-century, golden-age architecture, and plenty of canals – while mostly avoiding the hassles that go with the capital's often eccentric lifestyle. Zandvoort is the destination for Amsterdammers taking a day trip at the seaside. Both towns can be reached easily by train. If it's a sunny day, you might pack swimming gear and suntan lotion for Zandvoort beach.

Start from Amsterdam Centraal Station. There is a train to Haarlem every hour. For Zandvoort, you usually have to change trains at Haarlem on both the outward and return journeys, except in the high season when there are direct trains, too. The journey from Amsterdam to Haarlem takes only 15 minutes, and from Haarlem to Zandvoort another 15 minutes.

As soon as you arrive in **Haarlem**, take a good look around **Haarlem Station**. An Art Nouveau extravaganza dating from 1908, it can be considered a destination in its own right. The moderately priced **Station Restaurant**, situated in the former first-class waiting room, features pristine white tablecloths, conscientious service and, most importantly of all, fine cuisine. You might decide to stop here for lunch before going on to Zandvoort, or for dinner on the return journey.

When you emerge onto Stationsplein, walk down Kruisweg, which runs alongside the bus station, until you reach the Nieuwe Gracht. Cross over the canal and turn left along the waterside. At the Jansbrug, turn right for a short way on Jansstraat, then quickly left on Korte Jansstraat to the narrow canal called Bakenessergracht, which is lined by pretty gabled houses, where you turn right at the water.

The Oldest Church

The little alley called Kalverensteeg leads into Goudsmids Pleintje (Goldsmiths' Square), where the goldsmiths' guild was once based, and then to the **Waalse Kerk** (Walloon Church). This, Haarlem's oldest church, was erected in the 16th century by persecuted émigrés – Walloon Protestants and French Huguenots. The church is in the centre of Haarlem's old **Begijnhof**, whose tiny rooms, like their counterparts in Amsterdam, once housed religious lay

Left: an al fresco break in a Haarlem café
Right: cycling on the cobblestones is fun

women. Unlike that city's Begijnhof, however, they have now been put to a far less pious use: the Begijnhof constitutes Haarlem's **Rosse Buurt** (Red-Light District). Here you will find scantily-clad women waiting behind their windows for customers.

After circling the church, take Groene Buurt back to Bakenessergracht and turn right. Look for the white, crowned church spire of the **Bakenesserkerk** behind the roofs on your left; maybe you'll hear its bells as you pass. Bakenessergracht ends at the **River Spaarne**, where, if you wait, you're sure to see big canal boats passing under the Gravenstenenbrug. Cross over to the jetty from where the tour boats of **Woltheus Cruises** (tel: 023-535 7723) leave every hour for a cruise around the canals.

The Oldest Museum

Back on the other side of the bridge, you arrive at the distinguished, neo-classical facade of the **Teylers Museum** (16 Spaarne; Tues–Sat 10am–5pm, Sun 1–5pm; entrance fee) which, dating back to 1778, is the oldest museum in the Netherlands. The Teylers exhibits an eclectic array of items but emphasises science, particularly from the 19th century – everything from fossils and minerals to brass-mounted scientific instruments. You will also find paintings, drawings, medals and coins, and the museum's elegant interior would be worth seeing even if there were no exhibits.

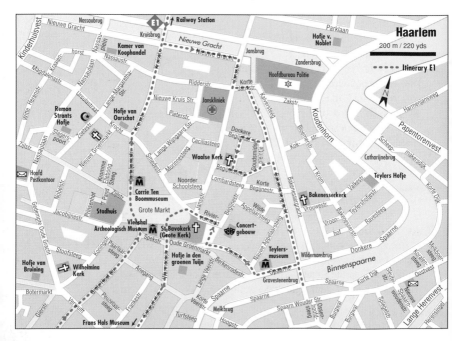

Next door to the Teylers is the **Waag** building (Weigh House), which dates back to 1597. It was built by the Flemish architect Lieven de Key, who designed many of Haarlem's most prominent buildings. It now houses the atmospheric **Herberg De Waag** restaurant (Thur–Tues 5pm–midnight).

Mozart Played Here

Take Damstraat to Oude Groenmarkt, where you will immediately see the imposing bulk of the **Sint-Bavokerk** (Saint Bavo's Church; Mon–Sat 10am–4pm; entrance fee) in front of you. Note the **Concertgebouw** (Concert Hall) on the corner of Klokhuisplein, then turn left into Rivierfischmarkt where, at No. 13, In Den Uiver is an old-style *proeflokaal* (tasting house). Work on the colossal, high-towered Sint-Bavokerk began in the mid-15th century under the direction of the Belgian architect Evert Spoorwater. Handel, Liszt and the 10-year-old Mozart all came to play the church's extraordinary, 1738 **Müller organ**. Inside the church is the tomb of the artist Frans Hals (1580–1666), who lived, worked and died in Haarlem. The square is lined with restaurants and cafés, many of which spread their open-air terraces out onto the street at the first sign of sunny weather.

Take Warmoesstraat at the side of the restaurant, then Schagchelstraat and Groot Heiligland. At 18 Warmoesstraat is the intimate restaurant **Jacobus Pieck** (tel: 023-532 6144), where you can order anything from a cup of coffee, via an intriguing sandwich and a health-food salad, to a Dutch or world-food main course. All emerge from the open kitchen in the hands of friendly waiters. You can dine in the garden in summer.

This is one of the most attractive residential neighbourhoods of Haarlem. The **Frans Hals Museum** (62 Groot Heiligland; Tues–Sat 11am–5pm, Sun noon–5pm; entrance fee), situated among a cluster of old houses originally built for Flemish retired gentlemen, is one of the city's foremost attractions. Hals is noted for paintings such as *The Laughing Cavalier* and *The Gypsy Girl*, but he earned his bread and butter painting portraits of members of the local musketeers' guild. Eight of his pictures hang in the museum, which also exhibits paintings by other Dutch masters, as well as collections of period furniture, fine silverware and ceramics. Look out for the beautiful 18th-century doll's house.

From the museum continue to the canal at the end of Groot Heiligland. Turn right, then second right on Grote Houtstraat, following the street's continuation, Grote Straat – both of which are major shopping streets – to the **Grote Markt**. On your right is the 16th-century **Vleeshal** (meat market),

Above Left: St Bavo's Church spire
Right: in the Frans Hals Museum

which now houses the city's **Archaeological Museum** (Wed–Sun 1–5pm; entrance free). On the Grote Markt is a sculpture of Laurens Coster, a 15th-century local hero, by the Mechelen artist Louis Royer. Haarlemmers will tell you that it was Coster, not Gutenberg, who invented the printing press. Work on the **Stadhuis** (Town Hall), began in the 14th century; today the building features a tapestry of the Crusades, dating from 1629.

If you want refreshments, **Grand Café Brasserie Fortuyn** at 23 Grote Markt is an ideal place for sitting on a terrace (in good weather) and watching the world go by. Leave the square by Bartel Jorisstraat, passing the ever-popular **Café 1900** (No. 10), with decor from that period. Continue on

Kruisstraat, past the 17th-century **Hofje van Oorschot**, to Kruisweg and back to Haarlem Station for the trip to the brassy North Sea resort of **Zandvoort**.

The beach

From Zandvoort Station it takes only five minutes to walk to the beach which, in summer, is lined with *paviljoenen* (temporary beach café-restaurants). Gays and naturists congregate at the south end of the long stretch of excellent sand.

Situated among the dunes just a stone's throw from the coast is **Circuit Park Zandvoort** (63 Burg van Alphenstraat) which, from 1952 to 1985, hosted the Dutch Formula One Grand Prix. Fans hope that what was once a highlight of the national sporting calendar will soon return; in the meantime the circuit still hosts less prestigious car and motorbike racing events.

Aficionados of a quite different type of sport will doubtless appreciate the many charms – roulette, blackjack and so forth – of **Holland Casino Zandvoort** (7 Badhuisplein; daily 1.30pm–3am; entrance fee) behind the central area of the promenade. One of 10 legal casinos in the country, it applies a formal dress code (collar and tie for men) and a minimum age (18). You will be expected to produce your passport if you want to gain entry.

Away from the beach but still on the seafront you might choose to tour the **Amsterdamse Waterleidingduinen** – rolling dunes that constitute part of Amsterdam's sea defences. You can roam on paths among the dunes on the sea side, and through woods on the inland side.

Zandvoort is not a particularly good place for shopping, but if you hit the centre of town you will find an array of places to eat, drink and shop. A large number of the shops concentrate on summer clothes, beach accessories and all types of sporting goods that complement the resort's outdoor lifestyle.

Above: in summer Zandvoort's cafés spill onto the pavements

2. THE IJSSELMEER BY BIKE   *(see map below)*

A day-long cycling tour to Hoorn following a narrow track between the polders and the IJsselmeer lake, returning to Amsterdam by train.

Start on the ferry that leaves from the rear of Centraal Station. The dykes and polders beside the IJsselmeer get very windy so wear appropriate clothing. This itinerary is a strenuous ride so various exit points are suggested.

It's a good idea to rent your bike on the day before undertaking this itinerary to facilitate an early start. (Try Bike City, Bloemgracht 68–70, near the Anne Frankhuis.) Cycle to Centraal Station and take the **Adelaarswegveer** (ferry) from the pier by the station, for the short trip to Amsterdam North *(see Itinerary 6: The Harbour, page 39)*. Follow the road directly ahead, Meeuwenlaan, to a roundabout, and turn right onto Nieuwendammerdijk. Opposite a small lake the road veers right onto Schellingwouderdijk, which twists and turns beside the water before becoming Durgerdammerdijk. Follow the dyke road along the tranquil IJsselmeer shore, always keeping the lake on your immediate right. The **IJsselmeer** was once a sea, the Zuiderzee, until the 1930s, when a barrier was constructed to protect the low-lying coastline.

A grandstand view

At **Durgerdam**, the pace of life slips down a gear or two. Typical of lakeside villages, Durgerdam huddles below the water level behind the protective dyke, with only its roofs peering over the top. Ride beside the houses or venture up to the dyke-top path, past **Uitdam**, with the sail-studded lake on your right and a grandstand view over the polders on your left.

Above: a classic polder landscape

Turn right at a T-junction onto the causeway leading to **Marken**. (If you're short of time or stamina, turn left instead to skip Marken which, though beautiful, represents a considerable diversion.) Marken is no longer an island – the causeway connects it to the mainland – but it remains insular. The green-and-white-painted houses of the village are clustered around a tiny harbour to the left of the car park. The remainder of the island is given over to farming. A white lighthouse stands at its tip and *boters* and *skûtsjes* (old-style Zuiderzee sailing ships), ply the waters offshore. For a *koffie en appelgebak met slagroom* (coffee and apple pie with cream) go to **De Taanderij**, a cosy harbour side café.

In the summer, you can take an excursion boat, the *Marken Express* (journey time: 25 minutes, frequent service), to Volendam, which means bypassing **Monnickendam** and saving yourself a fair amount of pedalling. Otherwise, retrace your route back across the causeway, and stay on the lake side road as far as Monnickendam. The harbour here has a vast array of pleasure craft, from little dinghies to gleaming, ocean-going luxury cruisers, plus fishing boats.

Volendam and Edam

Stick to the shore and pass through Katwoude on the way to **Volendam**. The populist face of Dutch tourism is on display here. Some of the locals still wear traditional costumes – you can have your picture taken wearing clogs and short jackets, or long, flowery aprons and milkmaid hats. Harbour-side fish-stalls do brisk business, especially with smoked IJsselmeer *paling* (eel). If by now you've had enough cycling, this is a good point from which to head back to Amsterdam. But if you still have energy to burn, go inland a short way from the lake dyke to **Edam**, a charming town famed for its *Edammer* cheese. This is another potential exit point – you can keep going west of Edam to nearby **Purmerend**, which has a railway station on the Amsterdam-Hoorn line. If you're game for more, turn right at the canal bridge at **Damplein** in the town centre, and right again to return to the IJsselmeer shore.

Ahead of you is a long, straight run north through the polders beside the lake. The little villages of **Warder**, **Etersheim** and **Scharwoude** are landmarks on the way to **Hoorn**. This, another of the IJsselmeer's emblematic places, is a living reminder of the traders and explorers from Zuiderzee towns in the past – South Africa's Cape Horn takes its name from Hoorn. The town wears its history on its sleeve – witness the care lavished on old sailors' houses, gabled merchants' villas, the Stadhuis (Town Hall) and churches.

It's worth visiting the beautiful inner harbour, the **Binnenhaven**, before taking a restorative drink at the **Hoofdtoren**, a 1532 harbour tower which is now an atmospheric bar and restaurant. Finally, follow the green signs, pointing first to the VVV (local tourism office), then to the station.

Above: traditional dress in Marken
Above Right: an old-fashioned touch in The Hague

3. THE HAGUE *(see map below)*

A day trip by train to The Hague to see the centres of political power, and to stroll along the seafront at the chic resort of Scheveningen.

From Amsterdam Centraal Station take the Inter City (IC) train to Den Haag Centraal Station. There are five trains every hour, and the journey takes 55 minutes.

The Hague is Holland's seat of government – Amsterdam is the capital. In contrast with Amsterdam's laid-back, anything-goes approach, The Hague

is elegant and refined. Commonly known as Den Haag (its official name is 's-Gravenhage), it seems less quintessentially Dutch than Amsterdam and, as befits the home of royalty, politicians and bureaucrats, it is well-heeled and a trifle smug.

A Monstrous Mall

Emerging from Centraal Station into the broad Koningin Julianaplein, you can't help but notice, to your right, the monstrous **Babylon** shopping mall and entertainment centre. Pick up a city-centre map from the VVV (local tourism office) on Babylon's ground floor then re-cross Koningin Julianaplein to the traffic lights beside the tram stop. Cross over to Herengracht and Korte Poten. To your left you should be able to see the top of the **De Resident** twin towers complex, part of a gargantuan urban-renewal project under the aegis of several top international architects.

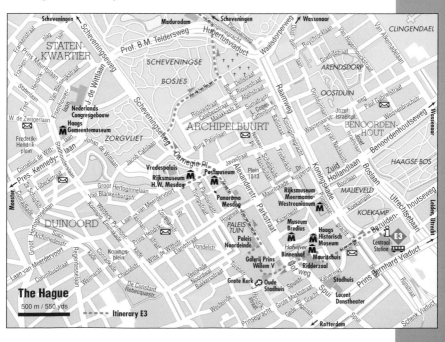

The Hague

500 m / 550 yds

- - - - - Itinerary E3

Keep straight on, to **Plein**, an economically named square (*plein* means square), with a statue of William I, Prince of Orange, presiding in the middle. At its northwest corner is Korte Vijverberg, on which, at No. 8, stands the **Mauritshuis** (Apr–Aug: Mon–Sat 10am to 5pm, Sun 11am–5pm; Sept–Mar: Tues–Sat 10am–5pm, Sun 11am–5pm). In this palace, dating from 1644, is a superb collection of paintings by Rembrandt, Vermeer, Hals, Brueghel, Rubens and other important artists. A 20th-century highlight here is Andy Warhol's portrait of Queen Beatrix.

Houses of Parliament

At the corner of Korte Vijverberg and Plein you will find the entrance to the **Binnenhof** (Inner Court) of the **Houses of Parliament** (Mon–Sat 10am–4pm; entrance fee). Here, in the 13th-century court of the Counts of Holland, is the magnificent, oak-roofed, Gothic **Ridderzaal** (Hall of the Knights), where the sovereign officially opens Parliament every year. Both of the bicameral Parliament's debating chambers, and the Prime Minister's office, are located here. Pass under the western arch to **Buitenhof**. To your right you will see the ornamental **Hof Vijver** lake, with an island and fountain in the middle.

Cross the road and walk to the far end of Buitenhof. On the left side is the graceful **Passage** shopping arcade. Straight ahead you will see the Dagelijkse Groenmarkt, with the **'t Goude Hooft** café-restaurant located in a 16th-century building at No. 13. (The interior was reconstructed in the 20th century following a fire.) If you stop here for lunch, the mussels are excellent, as is the terrace in good weather. A few steps past the restaurant brings you to

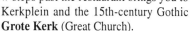

Kerkplein and the 15th-century Gothic **Grote Kerk** (Great Church).

Leave Kerkplein by Grote Halstraat beside the 1565 Renaissance-style **Oude Stadhuis** (Old Town Hall). Then take the pedestrian-only shopping streets, Oude Molstraat and Papestraat, to Noordeinde, where you turn left. On the road's left side is the neoclassical **Paleis Noordeinde** (Noordeinde Palace). This, the office of Queen Beatrix, is not open to the public. At 98 Noordeinde is **Van Hoogstraten**, an English bookstore and, at No. 121, **It Rains Fishes**, a smart seafood restaurant.

At the end of Noordeinde, cross over the canal to Zeestraat and **Panorama Mesdag**

Top: the Houses of Parliament's Inner Court. **Left:** the neoclassical Noordeinde Palace
Right: there's plenty to do and see in Scheveningen

(65 Zeestraat; Mon–Sat 10am–5pm, Sun noon–5pm; entrance fee). Painted in 1881, this is a restored, 120-metre (394-ft) circular panoramic painting of Scheveningen, The Hague's seaside resort. You may recall the fascinating panorama when you visit Scheveningen later in the day.

International Court of Justice

Continue to the end of Zeestraat, and cross over to Carnegieplein, on which stands the **Vredespaleis** (Peace Palace; guided tours Mon–Fri 10am, 11am, 2pm, 3pm, 4pm; entrance fee). Today the palace, built in the first decade of the 20th century with money donated by the Scottish-American philanthropist Andrew Carnegie, houses the International Court of Justice. If by now you have done enough walking, take tram No. 1 from Carnegieplein to Scheveningen.

There is one more place, a model city, that is worth walking to, but it is a fair distance away. Continue on Scheveningseweg, turn right on Arny van der Spuyweg, then left on Dr Aletta Jacobsweg, to arrive right opposite **Madurodam Miniature City** (175 Haringkade; Jan–Mar: daily 9am–6pm; Apr–June: daily 9am–8pm; Jul–Aug: daily 9am–10pm; entrance fee). This enchanting 1:25-scale Dutch city features working lights, bells that ring, planes that taxi on the runway, and trains that run. Children and adults alike love it.

To reach **Scheveningen** from here, take tram No. 9 from Madurodam and get off at Gevers Deynootplein beside the impressive, century-old **Kurhaus Hotel**. Take a walk along the seafront, and out onto the **pier**, where you are surrounded by the North Sea. The **Scheveningen Sea Life Centre** (13 Strandweg; Jul–Aug: daily 10am–8pm; Sept–Jun: daily 10am–6pm; entrance fee) is an aquarium with a glass tunnel surrounded by water, in which you can see sharks and other denizens of the deep in glorious proximity.

A little further along is **Beelden aan Zee** (Sculptures on the Seafront, 1 Harteveltstraat; Tues–Sun 11am–5pm; entrance fee), an open-air modern-sculpture park. In summer you can relax over a coffee or beer at one of the many beach cafés or, alternatively, at the **Kurhaus**. Afterwards take tram No. 1 or 9 back to Centraal Station for the return train journey to Amsterdam.

Leisure Activities

SHOPPING

Amsterdam is a great city for shopping but not in the same way as New York, London or Paris. Although it has plenty of upscale designer and department stores, the city's intimate, eccentric lifestyle is reflected in its more interesting shopping possibilities. These are to be found in offbeat speciality shops, highly individualistic outlets and in a diverse array of flourishing street markets. If you keep your eyes open in the course of this book's suggested itineraries and excursions, you will doubtless appreciate that the consumer options Amsterdam are boundless.

Dutch products that make good buys and souvenirs include the following: **flower bulbs** (but be warned that, to import these to some countries, you will be required to show a phytosanitary certificate); Delft and Makkum **pottery** (for high-quality originals, Delft products are labelled 'De Porcelyne Fles', their Makkum equivalents, 'Tichelaars'); Koninklijke Leerdam **crystal**; **pewter**; **cheese** from specialist shops; **chocolates** from Droste, Van Houten and Verkade; **antiques**; and **diamonds**.

If you are looking for a bargain, the most relevant words are *Solden* (Sales) and *Totale Uitverkoop* (Everything Must Go). Non-EU residents may be able to claim back value-added tax (BTW) paid on purchases. Shops announce their participation in this scheme with a sign in the window. Even if you don't see the sign, it's worth asking, particularly if you buy expensive items.

Thursday evening is *koopavond* (late-shopping), when most shops are open till 9pm. In recent years numerous shops have extended their opening hours to Sunday.

Kalverstraat

Kalverstraat is Amsterdam's most popular shopping thoroughfare. It is full of cheap and cheerful outlets, supplemented by a sprinkling of higher-priced designer stores. While the actual street begins at the Dam and runs to Muntplein, the shopping zone includes its continuation across the Dam in Nieuwendijk, and adjacent Rokin. The Dam features several department stores, including the **Bijenkorf** (Amsterdam's best), and **Peek & Cloppenburg**. Along the way is **Maison de la Bonneterie** and, at the far end of Kalverstraat, the **Vroom & Dreesman** (V&D) mid-range department store and **Hema** (Holland's answer to Woolworths).

Beyond the mass of clothes, sports and shoe shops, this district features a branch of **Waterstone's** bookshop chain, at 152 Kalverstraat, and, on the same subject, the **American Book Center** at No. 185. On Rokin, one of the most interesting shops is the **PGC Hajenius** tobacconist at No. 92–96. If you like your Havanas from a humidor, or want a traditional clay pipe for a souvenir, this is the place for you.

Pieter Cornelisz Hooftstraat

The best place for designer clothes is Pieter Cornelisz Hoofstraat – better known as the 'PC Hooft' *(see Itinerary 3, page 34)* – and the adjoining Van Baerlestraat. You will find this district in the Museum Quarter,

Left: one of many individual boutiques
Right: ceramics are always popular

not far from the rear of the Rijksmuseum. Some of the highly rated outlets on the PC Hooft include: **Azzurro Due**, **Edgar Vos**, **Jacques d'Ariège** and **McGregor**. Here you will also find a branch of the Belgian chocolatier **Godiva**.

Leidsestraat

Leidsestraat runs from Leidseplein, through Koningsplein, and on to Heiligeweg before it joins up with the southern end of Kalverstraat. It is actually an up-market extension of Kalverstraat, with outlets such as Esprit and Cartier. If you're looking for footwear, one of the city's most interesting options is **Shoe-Ba-Loo** at 7 Koningsplein.

Offbeat Shops and Boutiques

There are numerous offbeat stores and designer outlets throughout Amsterdam. The most central and convenient follow the route of the main city-centre canals and the lateral streets that connect the canals (among them the famous Negen Straatjes, or Nine Streets), beginning in the Jordaan and continuing to the Spui neighbourhood. From there they jump across Rokin to circumvent the periphery of the red-light district before fading out around Waterlooplein.

Among the most interesting of these shops are: **Animation Art**, 19 Berenstraat; **BLGK Edelsmeden**, 28 Hartenstraat; **Droomdoos**, 1 Oude Leliestraat; **Kitsch Kitchen Supermercado**, 8–12 Rozengracht; **Nieuws Innovations**, 297 Prinsengracht; **The Blue Gold Fish**, 17 Rozengracht; and **'t Winkeltje**, located at 228 Prinsengracht.

Markets

Amsterdam loves street markets. Some are permanent, others appear on a day or two each week. Among the best markets are: **Albert Cuyp Market**, Albert Cuypstraat (Mon–Sat); **Bio Market**, Noordermarkt, which specialises in organically grown fruit and vegetables (Sat); **Bloemenmarkt**, Singel, the famous flower market, where prices are competitive and the flowers excellent (Mon–Sat); **Garden Market**, Amstelveld (Mon); **Textile Market**, Noordermarkt (Mon morning); **Thorbecke Art Market**, Thorbeckeplein (Mar–Dec only: Sun); **Waterlooplein Rommelmarkt**, the city's premier flea market, where everything and anything goes.

Spiegelkwartier Antiques

The Spiegelgracht Canal near Leidseplein leads onto Nieuwe Spiegelstraat, which together have become an enclave of quality antiques shops.

Diamonds

Amsterdam prides itself on being the 'City of Diamonds'. There is a certain amount of marketing hype about this – Antwerp's diamond trade is worth six times as much. Still, a billion euros or so of annual sales add up to a sparkling business, and Amsterdam makes it fun to shell out for precious stones. You are unlikely to find much in the way of bargains, though.

Shops that were once associated with the now-defunct Amsterdam Diamond Foundation are reputable, and they offer tours in which you can see diamond cutting and polishing. The relevant shops are: **Amsterdam Diamond Centre**, 1–5 Rokin; **Coster**, 2–8 Paulus Potterstraat; **Gassan**, at 173–5 Nieuwe Uilenburgerstraat; **Stoeltie**, 13–17 Wagenstraat; and **Van Moppes**, at 2–6 Albert Cuypstraat.

Out of Town

You don't have to trudge around the city centre for shopping. For instance, the Amstelveen mall *(see Itinerary 8, Amsterdam by Tram, page 44)* is a 40-minute tram ride away from Centraal Station. Branches of **Vroom & Dreesman** and **Hema** are here, along with a range of designer outlets.

Above: the place to buy flower bulbs

EATING OUT

Given that Amsterdam is an adventurous, cosmopolitan city whose population includes a rainbow of ethnic minorities, it is not surprising that its restaurant scene constitutes a smorgasbord of international cuisine. They say you can eat in any language here, which is not far from the truth. The breadth of culinary options is matched by the quality, at all points on the price scale. Moreover, reflecting the Dutch insistence on getting a good return for every euro spent, restaurants tend to represent good value for money.

You should not have any trouble finding a decent place to eat. The old city centre is so thickly populated with restaurants it's a wonder that the residents have anywhere left to live. Although the dense clusters of restaurants around Leidseplein and Rembrandtplein contribute to the colourful atmosphere of both those neighbourhoods, they do not necessarily represent the best of the city's culinary offerings.

Dutch specialities to look out for include Zeeland mussels, raw herring, smoked eel, asparagus, *erwtensoep* (pea-and-ham soup) and *hutspot* (beef-and-vegetable stew), and Indonesian *saté* (grilled meat on skewers, with peanut sauce). Children in particular should sample the pancakes and *poffertjes* (mini-pancakes).

In general, any restaurant that serves meals cooked according to the Old Dutch style, even if it seems touristy, is a good bet. And, when the weather allows, dining al fresco on a restaurant terrace is recommended. If you are looking for a good, inexpensive meal, try an *eetcafé*, the best of which are traditional brown cafés. By contrast, the grand cafés are sometimes rather pretentious. For something a little more ethnic, try an Indonesian restaurant.

The price categories listed below are based on a three-course meal for two with a bottle or carafe of house wine:

€ = €40–75
€€ = €75–120
€€€ = €120–160

Most Amsterdam restaurants have a perfectly acceptable *dagschotel* or *dagmenu* (dish or menu of the day), that can cut up to 40 percent off the price of your meal.

Right: specialities of the day

Upscale
Café Américain
American Hotel, 97 Leidsekade
Tel: 020-556 3116
The city's beautiful people like to see and be seen at the landmark that is the Café Américain. The stylish venue – diners are surrounded by Art Deco and Art Nouveau – is complemented by the menu. €€

Excelsior
Hotel de l'Europe, 2–8 Nieuwe Doelenstraat
Tel: 020-531 1777
Another restaurant situated in a hotel, the Excelsior offers a smart, fashionable gastronomic experience, in a chandeliered salon with expansive windows overlooking the River Amstel. The menu is Dutch and Continental. €€€

La Rive
Amstel Hotel, 1 Professor Tulpplein
Tel: 020-622 6060
This intimate and elegant river side hotel restaurant specialises in elaborate French cuisine. Under the direction of ace chef Edwin Kats, the service, which is on the formal side, is flawless. €€€

Traditional
De Blonde Hollander
28 Leidsekruisstraat
Tel: 020-627 0521
A cheap and cheerful eatery, where diners eat in sociable proximity at large tables in a cosy setting. The dishes – stews, soups, steaks – are straightforward and wholesome, if not particularly exciting. €

Bodega Keyzer
96 Van Baerlestraat
Tel: 020-637 3737
Ideally located for the Concertgebouw, Bodega Keyzer has been serving fine cuisine since 1903, and counts classical musicians and conductors among its regulars. €€

Dorrius
Crowne Plaza Amsterdam City Centre Hotel, 5 Nieuwezijds, Voorburgwal
Tel: 020-620 0500
Traditional Dutch food in a wood-beamed setting carved out of 19th-century canal houses. Specialities include *hutspot* (stew), duck, deer, and lamb sausage. €€

Haesje Claes
273–5 Spuistraat
Tel: 020-624 9998
You don't get more homely than this old-fashioned restaurant, which fully merits the prized description *gezellig* (that cosy, welcoming, specifically Dutch quality). The steaks are particularly recommended. €–€€

Pancake Bakery
191 Prinsengracht
Tel: 020-625 1333
This converted 17th-century canal side warehouse does an enormous, typically Dutch, range of outsize savoury and sweet pancakes. Particularly recommended for children. €

D'Vijff Vlieghen
294 Spuistraat
Tel: 020-530 4060
D'Vijff Vlieghen (The Five Flies) wends its way through five old gabled houses, and six dining rooms, each with a different slant on Old Dutch style. €€

Brown-Café Style
De Belhamel
60 Brouwersgracht
Tel: 020-622 1095
De Belhamel looks like a brown café from the outside but the interior is much more elegant than most such places. Continental cuisine with a classical-music backdrop. €€.

De Magere Brug
81 Amstel
Tel: 020-622 6502
De Magere Brug is an old-fashioned neighbourhood restaurant that often caters to performers at the local Theater Carré. €

De Prins
124 Prinsengracht
Tel: 020-624 9382
There's no friendlier place in Amsterdam than De Prins, which might explain why, at peak times, you will probably have to wait for a free table. Moreover, the cuisine, which is both good and stylish, represents very good value for money. €

Above: traditional Dutch fare

Fashionable restaurants
Bordewijk
7 Noordermarkt
Tel: 020-624 3899
The cold grey-and-black décor at this trendy eatery just off Prinsengracht is almost painfully chic, and you might wonder if you're allowed to enjoy the food or simply remain content with making a fashion statement. Fortunately, the superb Franco-Mediterranean cuisine saves the day – you're allowed to enjoy it, after all. €€

Café De Kroon
17 Rembrandtplein
Tel: 020-625 2011
The Café De Kroon is arguably the finest of the grand cafés, for all its rather severe designer look, not least due to an excellent position overlooking Rembrandtplein. €–€€

Grand Café Luxembourg
24 Spuistraat
Tel: 020-620 6264
The Grand Café Luxembourg is, as its name suggests, possibly too smart for its own good. Nevertheless, it has earned its place as one of the smartest restaurants on the Amsterdam scene. Its menu includes a number of dishes taken from some of the city's favourite eateries. €–€€

Vertigo
Film Museum, 3 Vondelpark
Tel: 020-612 3021
Vertigo might seem like an incongruous name for a restaurant set in a basement but the reference – one of many that might appeal to film fans – is to the Alfred Hitchcock movie rather than any fear of heights. The food is Mediterranean-inspired and in good weather you can eat outdoors on one of the finest terraces in town. €€

Wildschut
1–3 Roelof Hartplein
Tel: 020-676 8220
This permanently trendy café-restaurant has a pavement terrace that is good for catching some late-afternoon sunshine, which might explain its popularity with after-hours office workers. The food ranges from bar snacks to well-prepared international dishes. €–€€

Right: coffee shops abound

Ethnic
Kantjil en de Tijger
291–3 Spuistraat
Tel: 020-620 0994
The menu and atmosphere are both cool and refined. The cuisine constitutes a kind of Indonesian nouvelle cuisine. €€

Morita-Ya
18 Zeedijk
Tel: 020-638 0756
Despite its cramped interior, this Japanese restaurant on the edge of the Red-Light District is excellent. The sushi is superb and, when they are not too busy, the staff might offer you tips on how to prepare it. €€

Nam Kee
111–113 Zeedijk
Tel: 020-624 3470
Chinese restaurants don't come much plainer than this one just off Nieuwmarkt, where the décor is so minimalist as to be non-existent. Nor do they come better, so there are often queues for a table. The food is authentic and the service is authentically rushed. €–€€

Rakang
29–31 Elandsgracht
Tel: 020-620 9551
Thai restaurants rarely feature in Amsterdam's hip scene, but this Jordaan example has not only made it and stayed there, but also gained a reputation for great, authentic food in the process. €–€€

Rose's Cantina
38–40 Reguliersdwarsstraat
Tel: 020-625 9797
Rose's is a Tex-Mex temple of fun that is virtually always busy, bustling and convivial.

The food is hardly top-notch, and your meal may take a long time to arrive, but you can pass the time with a jug or two of potent margaritas. €

Sama Sebo
27 Pieter Cornelisz Hooftstraat
Tel: 020-662 8146
Sama Sebo serves classic Indonesian fare, the authenticity of which is complemented by mats made from rushes and batik. Take your pick from the *rijsttafel* (rice table) – a selection of 20 or 30 little dishes that represent a cross-section of Indonesian cuisine. €€

Sherpa
58 Korte Leidsedwaarsstraat
Tel: 020-623 9495
This cosy restaurant serves up authentic Nepalese and Tibetan cuisine, with traditional mountain grills among the house specialities. €

Traiterie Grekas
311 Singel
Tel: 020-620 3590
The culinary offerings at this Greek restaurant compensate for the lack of space. There are only four tables, so you may have to settle for a takeaway. €

Vegetarian
Bolhoed
60–2 Prinsengracht
Tel: 020-626 1803
Bolhoed serves international dishes with a meat-free slant. The staff take an admirably breezy approach. You can eat on a terrace beside the canal in summer. €

Golden Temple
126 Utrechtsestraat
Tel: 020-626 8560
Some patrons come to the Golden Temple for the excellent salad buffet, others for the main courses – featuring creative Indian, Middle Eastern and Mexican cuisine. €

Seafood
Le Pêcheur
32 Reguliersdwarsstraat
Tel: 020-624 3121
If seafood were art, then this upscale restaurant would be something of a meticulous masterpiece, with prices to match. There are few more romantic places in town to dine on a summer evening than in the mansion's flower-bedecked back garden; at all other times the graceful interior salon takes some beating. €€

Haarlem
Ma Brown's
31–33 Nieuwe Groenmarkt
Tel: 023-531 5829
Given the traditional British nature of Ma Brown's cuisine, the food is surprisingly sophisticated. Afternoon teas are served on the first and third Sunday of the month. €€€

De Pêcherie Haarlem aan Zee
10 Oude Groenmarkt
Tel: 023-531 4848
Situated just off the Grote Markt, this restaurant is an excellent choice for lovers of seafood. The marine decor is redolent of a good-weather day on the beach at nearby Zandvoort. €€

The Hague
't Goude Hooft
13 Groenmarkt
Tel: 070-350 2434
A somewhat old-fashioned, rustic restaurant situated in the heart of The Hague, 't Goude Hooft underwent a modern reconstruction following a fire. Its extensive menu covers everything from bar snacks to full-scale traditional Dutch meals. €–€€

Above: a toast to some of the best beer in the world
Right: a romantic night setting

NIGHTLIFE

Amsterdam is well-known for its vibrant nightlife – a scene that runs the gamut from the high culture of sophisticated venues for classical music, opera, theatre and dance, to the notoriously erotic and often sleazy dens of the Red-Light District. In between are the numerous – and frequently bohemian – haunts of contemporary café society, plus lots of cabaret venues, nightclubs and discos, featuring the very latest in hip-hop, techno, garage and other current sounds for a young crowd.

Highlights of the regular September–May cultural season include the Holland Festival, which takes place every June. This festival is associated with events in other cities – notably The Hague, Rotterdam and Utrecht. In July and August, the somewhat avant-garde Amsterdam Arts Adventure event attracts creative types from throughout the country.

The local theatre scene is excellent, but you are unlikely to appreciate it unless you are conversant with Dutch – the language spoken in virtually all local productions. If you are a real theatre aficionado however, it is worth checking the listings and programmes during your visit, as there may well be one or two performances in English.

Amsterdam's major cinemas screen international films in their original language (with subtitles). Given the ubiquity of Hollywood productions, English-speaking cinema-goers can enjoy movies in their own language.

The nightlife venues listed in this section cover the main focal points of entertainment in Amsterdam and beyond, but there are plenty of other options on offer. For arts and entertainment listings, the VVV (local tourism association) publishes the monthly English-language magazine *Amsterdam Day by Day*. There are VVV offices inside the Centraal Station building, outside the station on Stationsplein, and also at 1 Leidseplein (tel: 0900-400 4040).

You might have a look at the free, Dutch-language, monthly *Uitkrant* and several other publications published by AUB (Amsterdams Uit Buro, 21 Kleine Gartmanplantsoen, tel: 020-621 1211; www.aub. nl). Also look out for the free *Amsterdam Weekly*, which has some details of what's on and where, and can be found at numerous cafés and other venues around town.

Classical Music
Beurs van Berlage
1 Beursplein
Tel: 020-521 7520
The Beurs van Berlage, the beautiful old Stock Exchange building near the Dam, dates from 1903. Transformed into a twin-hall concert venue, it is today the home of the Netherlands Philharmonic Orchestra and the Netherlands Chamber Orchestra, both of which are worth going to hear.

Concertgebouw
2–6 Concertgebouwplein
Tel: 020-626 6866
The prosaically named Concertgebouw (Concert Building) is one of the world's most illustrious concert halls. The city's leading venue for classical music, it is home to the renowned Concertgebouw Orchestra.

The Hague
Dr Anton Philips Concertzaal
150 Spui
Tel: 070-360 9810
Home to The Hague's Residentie Orchestra.

Churches
Among the churches featuring outstanding organs – which are often utilised for recitals and chamber-music concerts – are these:

Engelse Kerk
48 Begijnhof
Tel: 020-624 9665

Nieuwe Kerk
Dam
Tel: 020-638 6909

Oude Kerk
Oudekerksplein
Tel: 020-625 8284

Waalse Kerk
Walenpleintje (at Oudezijds Achterburgwal)
Tel: 020-623 2074

Opera and Dance
Muziektheater
3 Amstel (at Waterlooplein)
Tel: 020-625 5455
The once-controversial Muziektheater is now an established star of the Dutch cultural scene. It is home to both the Netherlands Opera and the Netherlands Dance Theatre.

Stadsschouwburg
26 Leidseplein
Tel: 020-624 2311
The opera and dance productions staged here tend to be more avant-garde than the shows at the Muziektheater.

The Hague
Lucent Dans Theater
152 Spui
Tel: 070-360 4930
This is a modern venue where the esteemed Nederlands Dans Theater's three troupes perform.

Theatre
Carré
115–25 Amstel
Tel: 0900-252
This large theatre situated on the banks of the Amstel features well-known international music acts. The musicals may be in Dutch or in English, with many of the latter performed by touring companies from London and New York.

Nieuwe de la Mar Theater
404 Marnixstraat
Tel: 020-530 5302
Mainstream theatre, with plays usually in Dutch but occasionally in English.

Theater Bellevue
90 Leidsekade
Tel: 020-530 5301
Plays on an intimate scale. Seasonal programmes include English-language productions from time to time.

Dance Clubs
Akhnaton
25 Nieuwezijds Kolk
Tel: 020-624 3396
Offers an eclectic range of music, attracting a diverse crowd. Live jazz and salsa top the bill.

Dansen bij Jansen
11–13 Handboogstraat
Tel: 020-620 1779
This is a consistently popular student club. It manages to maintain its appeal with the ever-changing, youthful in-crowd.

Above: the Muziektheater is an excellent venue for opera and dance

nightlife

Melkweg
234a Lijnbaansgracht
Tel: 020-531 8181
Located in a former dairy factory, the Melkweg (Milky Way) is a long-established venue which is something of a relic from the flower-power, marijuana-fuelled days of the 1960s. Now the hippie aesthetic has given way to multimedia chic, and the Melkweg features a dance floor, a theatre, a lecture hall and a cinema.

Odeon
460 Singel
Tel: 020-624 9711
An elegant 17th-century canal house on Singel has been converted into a dance club and café, to cater for a mixed, but invariably smart clientèle.

Pacific Parc
Westergasfabriek
6–10 Haarlemmerweg
Tel: 020-488 7778
Dance to funky Latin and hip-hop rhythms at this trendy spot in a sprawling, redeveloped gasworks complex situated to the west of Centraal Station.

Seymour Likely Lounge
161 Nieuwezijds Voorburgwal
Tel: 020-420 5663
This rather unusually named venue offers appropriately hip dance music in an avant-garde location.

Jazz and Blues
Alto Jazz Café
115 Korte Leidsedwarsstraat
Tel: 020-626 3249
One of the city's most popular and friendly jazz venues.

Bimhuis
3 Piet Heinkade
Tel: 020-788 2188
Cool and laid-back, Bimhuis features modern jazz and improvised music at its shiny new venue on the waterfront.

Bourbon Street
6 Leidsekruisstraat
Tel: 020-623 3440
Bourbon Street is highly recommended for those who like their jazz to be 'straight ahead' or mainstream.

Maloe Melo
163 Lijnbaansgracht
Tel: 020-420 4592
Mellow blues played nightly in a suitably smoky atmosphere.

Rock and Pop Concerts
Amsterdam ArenA
1 ArenA Boulevard
Bijlmermeer (Amsterdam Zuidoost)
Tel: 020-311 1444
Since it opened in 1996, the quite stupendous stadium of the Ajax Amsterdam football team has become a venue for big-name concerts from time to time.

Experimental Music
Muziekgebouw aan 't IJ
1 Piet Heinkade
Tel: 020-788 2000
Located on the waterfront just east of Centraal Station, this large modern venue is the place to go for the latest in pioneering musical sounds from around the world.

Cabaret
Boom Chicago
Leidseplein Theater, 12 Leidseplein
Tel: 020-423 0101
Fast-paced comedy theatre – usually in English – that satirises the leading international news of the day.

Left: Damrak, near Centraal Station

Casinos

Holland Casino Amsterdam
64 Max Euweplein
Tel: 020-521 1111
The city's only legal casino. Formal dress and passport for entry. Roulette, blackjack, punto banco (a version of baccarat) and poker. Or feed the slot machines.

Holland Casino Zandvoort
7 Badhuisplein
Tel: 023-574 0574
Like the Amsterdam branch but on the coast.

Cinemas

Bellevue
400 Marnixstraat
Tel: 0900-1458
Two screens in a street off Leidseplein.

Calypso
402 Marnixstraat
Tel: 0900-1458
Two-screen neighbour of the Bellevue.

City
15–19 Kleine Gartmanplantsoen
Tel: 0900-1458
Seven screens not far from Leidseplein.

The Movies
161 Haarlemmerdijk
Tel: 020-638 6016
Alternatives to Hollywood blockbusters.

Tuschinski
26–34 Reguliersbreestraat
Tel: 0900-1458
Six-screen cinema in a building whose fine Art Deco interior is itself worth an Oscar. Just off Rembrandtplein.

Brown Cafés

Café Chris
42 Bloemstraat
Tel: 020-624 5942
Located not far from Westermarkt, this café dates from 1624. Today's clientele, like much of the city, is fairly bohemian.

De Druif
83 Rapenburgerplein
Tel: 020-624 4530
Situated on the waterfront in the Oosterdok area, this popular local café is an institution, having opened in 1631.

Hoppe
18–20 Spui
Tel: 020-420 4420
Friendly, popular café from 1670.

In de Wildeman
3 Kolksteeg
Tel: 020-638 2348
In an alley off Nieuwezijds Voorburgwal, this 1690 brown café, originally a liqueur distillery, has an extensive range of beers.

't Smalle
12 Egelantiersgracht
Tel: 020-623 9617
Pavement and canal-side terraces.

Trendy Cafés

Dante
320 Spuistraat
Tel: 020-638 8839
Includes an art gallery where, every month, a new modern-art exhibition is displayed.

Kanis & Meiland
127 Levantkade
Tel: 020-418 2439
Unless you speak Dutch, or say it quickly, the clever pun in this brown café's name might not be clear – it's on KNSM Eiland (Island) in the redeveloped eastern harbour, and has a fine waterside terrace on a former dock to prove it.

Schiller
36 Rembrandtplein
Tel: 020-624 9864
Friendly, trendy temple of good taste.

Left: preparing a restorative beverage

CALENDAR OF EVENTS

March
In honour of the 1345 Miracle of the Host, Catholics parade in the *Stille Omgang* (Silent Procession), beginning at the Dam on the nearest Sunday to the 15th.
For details of the **Amsterdam Blues Festival** at De Meervaart, tel: 020-410 7720.
Keukenhof Garden at Lisse is open for the **tulip season** (Mar–May).

April
On **Good Friday**, the Concertgebouw Orchestra plays Bach's *The Passion According to Saint Matthew* in its concert hall.
National Museum Weekend (usually on a mid-month weekend) features free or reduced-rate entry to most city museums.
Koninginnedag (the Queen's official birthday) on the 30th is celebrated throughout the country. A street market and music festival bring Amsterdam to a standstill. Wear orange.

May
Bevrijdingsdag (Liberation Day) on 5 May celebrates the defeat of the Nazis. The revelries in Amsterdam are comparable to those on *Koninginnedag*.

June
The Vondelpark's open-air **theatre season** runs from June–Sept.
The **Holland Festival**, a month of music, theatre, opera, film and dance, focuses on Amsterdam, The Hague, Rotterdam and Utrecht. For details, tel: 020-627 6566.
The **Amsterdam Roots Festival** brings world music, dance, films, exhibitions and workshops to the Melkweg, on variable dates. For more information, tel: 020-531 8181.
Kunst rai (Arts RAI) at the RAI Exhibition centre (variable dates) showcases the art of a different country every year. For details, contact the RAI, tel: 020-549 1212.

July
Cultural events under the umbrella of the **Arts Adventure** programme take place in July and August. The idea is to extend the cultural season into these hitherto dormant months, when the city is full of tourists. Informal music, theatre and dance events are frequently held

at open-air venues. For details contact the AUB (Amsterdam Uit Buro), tel: 0900-0191.

August
The resort of Zandvoort swings to the sound of live jazz in its **Jazz Behind the Beach** festival, usually held in the mid-week of August at various venues in the town.

September
The *Bloemencorso* (Flower Parade) begins in Aalsmeer and ends in Amsterdam, usually in the first week of the month.
The **Jordaan Festival**, a loosely-structured series of musical and performance events, takes place in this Amsterdam district in the first two weeks of the month.
The **Amsterdam City Marathon** usually takes place at the end of the month.

November
On the Saturday nearest to 17 November, the **Arrival of Sinterklaas** (St Nicholas) is marked by a procession from Prins Hendrikkade to the city centre, featuring Nicolaas's helper, Zwarte Piet (Black Peter).

December
The **Sinterklaas Festival**, on 5 December – St Nicholas's Eve (also known as *pakjesavond*, or packages, evening) – is the traditional Dutch time for exchanging Christmas gifts, though 25 December is also now celebrated too.

Right: the sound of jazz

Practical Information

GETTING THERE

By Air

Amsterdam's Schiphol Airport, some 14km (9 miles) southwest of the city, is widely considered to be among the world's best. KLM Royal Dutch Airlines, owned by Air France, is the 'national' carrier. Most major international airlines fly to Amsterdam, and there are direct or connecting flights from (among other places) London and other UK cities, Dublin, New York, Los Angeles, Toronto, Sydney, Auckland, Johannesburg, Bombay, Singapore and Tokyo. For flight information, tel: 0900-0141 or visit www.schiphol.nl.

There is a 24-hour rail service from Schiphol to Centraal Station, with up to six trains an hour at peak times. Trains also leave, though less frequently, for Amsterdam RAI Station (for the giant congress and exhibition centre) and Amsterdam Zuid/WTC (South/World Trade Centre) Station. In all three cases, the journey time is about 20 minutes.

Taxis to the city centre depart from a rank in front of Schiphol Plaza. Connexxion operates a hotel shuttle bus from the airport, which serves 16 city-centre hotels (all of which are close to many other hotels), every 10–30 minutes from 6am to 9pm.

By Rail

There are regular international services to Centraal Station from Paris, Brussels, Cologne, Berlin and cities in eastern Europe, Switzerland and Italy. In addition, the Thalys high-speed train connects the city with Brussels, Cologne and Paris (reservations mandatory).

By Road

Four EU-designated motorways converge on the city from Belgium and Germany: the E19, E22, E35 and E231.

By Sea

DFDS Seaways operates a car ferry service with vessels sailing every second day between Newcastle and IJmuiden near Amsterdam; P&O Ferries has one sailing a day between Hull and Rotterdam Europoort; and Stena Line has two sailings a day between Harwich and Hoek van Holland near Rotterdam.

TRAVEL ESSENTIALS

When to Visit

The best times for a trip to Amsterdam is in spring, summer and early autumn (Apr–Oct). The weather is at its best and the museums and other attractions have longer opening hours. Spring is the time to see the glorious tulip displays in the nearby bulb fields. Winter can also be good, particularly if the canals freeze: bring your skates and see the city of canals in a different guise.

Visas and Passports

EU citizens do not need a visa. Citizens of most other European countries, the US, Canada, Australia, New Zealand, Japan and some other places do not need a visa for stays of up to three months. Citizens of other countries must have a visa. If in doubt, check with the Dutch embassy or consulate in your home country, or country of departure, or with your travel agent or airline.

Customs

There are no currency restrictions. EU citizens can import for personal use up to 800 cigarettes, 400 cigars, or 400g tobacco; 90 litres of wine; 10 litres of spirits.

Left: canal boats give a fine perspective
Right: a much faster mode of transport

Non-EU citizens can import duty-free a maximum of: 200 cigarettes, 50 cigars, or 50g of tobacco; 2 litres of wine, or 1 litre of spirits. If purchasing flower bulbs you should be aware that the majority of countries forbid the import of flower bulbs without an official phytosanitary certificate – many vendors sell bulbs with a certificate on the label.

Weather

The climate is generally temperate. July and August can be hot, but even in summer, Amsterdam, benefitting from its proximity to the North Sea, often enjoys a cooling breeze, and occasionally some rain.

Winters are sometimes cold enough for the canals to freeze over to the extent that ice-skaters can glide across them. The average summer temperature is 16°C (60°F), although it can rise to 30°C (86°F). In winter the average temperature is 3°C (37°F), but it can fall to -20°C (-4°F).

Clothing

Even in summer it's a good idea to bring a sweater or cardigan because the evenings can be cool. Moreover, due to Amsterdam's proximity to the sea, the weather can change quickly. An umbrella is a vital accessory at almost any time.

Warm clothes are essential in winter. In most situations, even if dining at a high-class restaurant or attending the opera, casual outfits are acceptable. Businesspeople often dress informally; Dutch business people tend to adopt a more stylish appearance than many of their foreign counterparts.

Electricity

The unit of electricity in the Netherlands is 220 volts AC. Hotels may have a 110-volt or 120-volt outlet for shavers.

Time

The country operates on Central European Standard Time, with Daylight Saving Time coming into play from late March to late October. (Daylight Saving Time is GMT plus one hour in winter, plus two hours in summer.) For most of the year, the Netherlands is one hour ahead of the UK, and six hours ahead of the US's Eastern Standard Time.

Right: a city of fine architectural detail

GETTING ACQUAINTED

Geography

Amsterdam, like most of the Netherlands, is uniformly flat and lies below sea level – dykes protect the land from the ravages of the North Sea. The Dam district constitutes the heart of the city. North of the Dam is Centraal Station, which is also the main tram, bus and metro terminus. A horseshoe of concentric canals – Singel, Herengracht, Keizersgracht and Prinsengracht – forms a semi-circle around the Dam, culminating at the River Amstel in the east.

Government and Economy

The city council is headed by a mayor whose power invariably entitles him to set his stamp on the city's social and economic affairs. Don't get carried away by Amsterdam's reputation for free living. Nowadays, that anything-goes lifestyle is more a product of the residents' wealth and liberalism than of hippie values and soft drugs.

As a result of assiduous promotion and heavy investment, the Amsterdam-Schiphol Airport district has become a booming enterprise zone, as can be seen from the extensive suburban business developments. Any number of multinational corporations have located their European headquarters and distribution operations here.

Religion

The Netherlands is predominantly Calvinist, with the Dutch Reformed Church being the most popular denomination. There is a substantial Roman Catholic minority (or majority in the south). But if you visit any

church in Amsterdam during a Sunday service you will find that religion is honoured more often in the breach than the observance.

How Not to Offend

It is hard to offend Amsterdammers, whose approach to life is that whatever works for you is okay by them. But even this live-and-let-live attitude has its limits. The locals don't like boorish, loud and aggressive behaviour, nor do they take kindly to being treated like servants. Like the majority of Dutch people they are proud of their nation – if not in a shallow, flag-waving sense – and don't like too much criticism of its ways.

Avoiding Trouble

You certainly should not trust the junkie in the Red-Light District who wants to take a photo of you with your own camera, nor should you give credence to most of the hard-luck stories you may hear at Centraal Station from people whose money has mysteriously vanished and who needs someone to pay for their ticket home. Watch out for pickpockets in all busy places, especially at Centraal Station and on crowded buses and trams.

Population

The population of Amsterdam stands at about 750,000, almost half of whom are either foreigners or from ethnic minorities. The old Dutch colonies of Indonesia and Surinam used to be the main sources of immigration. Nowadays, Amsterdam is a real melting pot, with immigrants from many countries.

MONEY MATTERS

Currency

The unit of currency in the Netherlands is the euro (€).There are 100 cents in a euro. Notes come in denominations of €5, €10, €20, €50, €100, €200 and €500. There are also 1-cent, 2-cent, 5-cent, 10-cent, 20-cent, €1 and €2 coins.

Credit Cards and Cheques

The major international credit and charge cards are accepted by a wide range of businesses. Travellers' cheques should be

exchanged for euros at banks, foreign exchange offices, or hotels.

Cash Machines

There are automatic cash-dispensers (ATMs) dotted all over the city. Many can be accessed by foreign bank cards and credit cards, some also by the major charge cards.

Tipping

Taxis, most restaurants, hairdressers, etc include a tip in the bill as a service charge. Staff still appreciate a tip of 5–10 percent for good service, although you won't be publicly humiliated for not leaving one. At many public toilets you have to deposit 30–50 cents in the attendant's saucer.

Taxes

Non-EU residents are entitled to a refund on the value-added tax (BTW) paid on purchases of €137 or more in one shop on one day. The goods must be exported from the EU within three months. Ask for a tax-free shopping receipt when you pay, and a leaflet that explains the scheme.

Money Changers

The 'commission' charged by some money-changing establishments may leave you with the feeling that you have been mugged. The GWK (Grenswisselkantoor) exchanges at airports, main railway stations, and some border motorway services offer the best deals. Banks are also reliable. In other locations, including hotels, ask about the rates and commission in advance.

Above: a welcoming taxi driver

GETTING AROUND

Walking

The best way to get around in Amsterdam is by foot, with public transport – especially trams – and bicycles for ancillary back-up. There are plenty of quiet streets and canal sides for getting away from the crowds and traffic.

Taxis

Officially, you are not allowed to wave down taxis in the street, but nowadays they usually stop if you do. Your best bet is either to wait at one of the taxi ranks around the city, for example at Centraal Station, the Dam, Leidseplein and Rembrandtplein, or tel. Taxi Centrale, tel: 020-677 7777 or 0900-677 7777.

Public Transport

The efficient public transport network of trams, buses and metro trains operated by GVB Amsterdam provides a bewildering array of fare options, the simplest of which is the *dagkaart* (day ticket), which gives unlimited use on the day – and night – of purchase. You can also buy a *strippenkaart* (strip ticket) with 8, 15 or 45 strips (the more strips, the less each one costs) which must be punched on the vehicle, by machine, driver or conductor.

The city is divided into public-transport zones. Punch one strip more than the number of zones in which you will be travelling – two strips for one zone, etc. The ticket is valid for unlimited transfers for one hour after the time stamped on it. Although you can buy tickets on trams and buses, they are cheaper at rail and metro ticket counters, newsagents and VVV (local tourism offices).

By the end of 2008 the national *OV-chipkaart*, an electronic card in use in Amsterdam from 2006, will replace all other public Dutch transport tickets. The card is topped up with euros, and the fare is deducted when the card is inserted into an electronic reader. During the transition period, strip tickets will remain valid.

The leaflet *Around Amsterdam: Visitor's Guide by Public Transport* gives useful information on how to get around the city and its environs by public transport.

Tram/Bus

There are 17 tram routes, 12 of which begin and end at Centraal Station. The routes are complemented by extensive urban and regional bus services. The lives of locals and visitors alike are made easier by maps of the city's public transport network that are posted at most tram and bus stops.

Metro/Train

There is a fast, modern metro service to outlying housing schemes and the southern suburbs. This is not of much use for getting around within the city centre. The train service is good for destinations beyond the city, but less so in the city itself.

Driving

Amsterdam has taken preventive measures to stem the flow of traffic into the old city centre. Parking is expensive, and illegally parked cars are clamped or towed away by the hyperefficient parking authority. In short, it is not a good idea to bring your car.

Neither is hiring a car a good way to see the city's attractions. But if you do choose this option, try either of the following:
• Avis: Schiphol Airport and 380 Nassaukade, tel: 0800-235 2847 or 020-683 6061.
• Budget: Schiphol Airport and 121 Overtoom, tel: 0900-1576 or 020-612 6066.
• Europcar: Schiphol Airport and 197 Overtoom, tel: 070-381 1812 or 020-683 2123.
• Hertz: Schiphol Airport and 333 Overtoom, tel: 020-201 3512.

Cycling

Hire bikes from some hotels, train stations or:
• MacBike, 2 Mr Visserplein, tel: 020-620 0985 and 12 Stationsplein, tel: 020-620 0985;
• Damstraat Rent-a-Bike, 20–22 Damstraat, tel: 020-625 5029.

Right: informal marketing for bike-hire

On the Water

In addition to taking tours by canal boat and water-bike, you can take advantage of the canals *qua* thoroughfares. To get around the city by canal boat, try one of the following:
* Canal Bus, tel: 020-623 9886, operates two city-centre routes.
* Museumboot, tel: 020-530 1090, connects some of the major museums by boat.
* Watertaxi, tel: 020-535 6363.

HOURS AND HOLIDAYS

Business Hours

Banks are open Mon–Fri 9am–4 or 5pm. Shops are usually open Mon–Sat 8.30 or 9am–6pm, with late-night shopping on Thursday until 9pm. Numerous shops are also open on Sunday, while some stay closed on Monday mornings. There are plenty of *avondwinkels* (local late-night shops) and 'corner stores' that stay open until 10pm or even later.

Public Holidays

New Year	1 January
Good Friday	variable
Easter Monday	variable
Koninginnedag	(Queen's Birthday) 30 April
Ascension Day	6th Thursday after Easter
Whit Monday	7th Monday after Easter
Christmas Day	25 December
Boxing Day	26 December

Market Days

Albert Cuyp Market (general): Albert Cuyp-straat, Mon–Sat.
Art Market: Thorbeckeplein, Mar–Dec: Sun.
Bio Market (organic fruit and vegetables): Noordermarkt, Sat.
Bloemenmarkt (flowers): Singel, Mon–Sat.
Garden Market: Amstelveld, Sun.
Textiles and Garment Market: Noordermarkt, Mon 9am–1pm
Flea Market (antiques and second-hand books): Waterlooplein, Mon–Sat.
Stamps and Coins Market: Nieuwezijds Voorburgwal (behind the Royal Palace), Wed and Sat, 9am–1pm.

Right: Café Américain at the American Hotel

ACCOMMODATION

Hotels

Amsterdam is well served by accommodation options in all price categories. In recent years the emphasis has been on the top end of the market – a trend that the municipality has been trying to reverse. At peak times in summer, and during the spring tulip season, it can be difficult to find rooms in low- and moderately-priced hotels, so book your accommodation in advance if possible. Should you arrive at such times without a room, your best bet is to go to the VVV (local tourism office) at Centraal Station: there are two offices here – one inside, the other outside the station – and the staff at both should be able to find a room and make reservations for you.

The price categories listed below are for a double room at roughly the following rates:
€ = €40–75
€€ = €75–150
€€€ = €150–250
€€€€ = over €250

Amstel Inter-Continental Amsterdam
1 Professor Tulpplein
Tel: 020-622 6060
Fax: 020-622 5808
www.intercontinenti.com
Built in 1867, the Amstel overlooks the River Amstel. Replete with marble, chandeliers and oceans of genuine Delft blue porcelain, it constitutes the ultimate in luxury. Its French La Rive restaurant has earned two prestigious Michelin stars. €€€€

Amsterdam American Hotel
97 Leidsekade
Tel: 020-556 3000
Fax: 020-556 3001
www.amsterdamamerican.com
A monument protected by the city on account of its Art Nouveau architecture, this hotel is also a testament to style. The staff's laid-back approach makes it popular with a wide range of people. A visit to its Café Américain is recommended. €€€€

Hôtel de l'Europe
2–8 Nieuwe Doelenstraat
Tel: 020-531 1777
Fax: 020-531 1778
www.leurope.nl
An elegant riverside hotel dating from 1896 with a distinctive red-and-white facade and a grand sense of style. The plush guest rooms have modern furnishings and amenities. The Excelsior restaurant is one of the most highly regarded in town. €€€€

NH Barbizon Palace
59–72 Prins Hendrikkade
Tel: 020-556 4564
Fax: 020-624 3353
www.nh-hotels.com
A superbly equipped hotel built alongside old canal houses opposite Centraal Station. The ideal option if you are looking for more than just a touch of modern luxury. €€€€

NH Grand Hotel Krasnapolsky
9 Dam
Tel: 020-554 9111
Fax: 020-622 8607
www.nh-hotels.com
Founded in 1866 but now modernised, the Kras is a local institution. Its Winter Garden restaurant is the epitome of Victorian-era elegance. Fine location at the Dam. €€€€

Estheréa
303–309 Singel
Tel: 020-624 5146
Fax: 020-623 9001
www.estherea.nl
With its beautiful canal-side location, the Estheréa combines old Amsterdam charm and 21st-century facilities. One of the best value-for-money options in the city. €€€

NH Schiller
26–36 Rembrandtplein
Tel: 020-554 0700
Fax: 020-624 0098
www.nh-hotels.com
As much an art gallery as a hotel, the Schiller was built in the *fin-de-siècle* period by an artist who filled it with his own creations and those by artists he particularly liked. The wood-panelled Café Schiller has long been one of the city's trendy hangouts. €€€

Pulitzer
315–331 Prinsengracht
Tel: 020-523 5235
Fax: 020-627 6753
www.luxurycollection.com
A terrace of 17th- and 18th-century canal houses converted into a hotel of charm and character. The furnishings are beautiful, the bedrooms – overlooking canals or gardens – sophisticated. The Rendezvous Lounge restaurant is appropriately classy. €€€

Radisson SAS
17 Rusland
Tel: 020-520 8300
Fax: 020-520 8200
www.radissonsas.com
Set deep in the heart of Old Amsterdam, this stylish Scandinavian hotel offers an eclectic range of designs in its rooms. €€€–€€€€

Victoria
1–5 Damrak
Tel: 020-627 1166
Fax: 020-627 4259
www.parkplazaeurope.com
Well-located opposite Centraal Station and impervious to the street noise. A plush, option, full of character. €€€

Ambassade
335–53 Herengracht
Tel: 020-555 0222
Fax: 020-555 0277
www.ambassade-hotel.nl
An hospitable, exclusive hotel created from a series of 17th- and 18th-century canal side houses, the Ambassade features plenty of antiques and paintings, and steep – in some cases spiral – staircases. Especially popular with visiting writers. €€

Amsterdam-De Roode Leeuw
93–94 Damrak
Tel: 020-555 0666
Fax: 020-620 4716
www.hotelamsterdam.nl
This fine, medium-sized hotel, conveniently situated near Centraal Station, opened in 1911 but has been thoroughly modernised. The hotel's De Roode Leeuw is one of the city's best Dutch restaurants. €€

Amsterdam Wiechmann
328 Prinsengracht
Tel: 020-626 3321
Fax: 020-626 8962
www.hotelwiechmann.nl
The laid-back American owner and his Dutch wife have turned this rambling old canalhouse hotel into one of the city's most welcoming addresses. You can't beat the location, and the rates are reasonable. €€

Best Western Eden
144 Amstel
Tel: 020-530 7888
Fax: 020-624 2946
www.edenhotelgroup.com
This moderately-priced river-side hotel has 410 rooms, so it might be a good bet when other hotels are fully booked. And it retains much of the character of the 17th-century merchants' homes from which it was created. Guest rooms are furnished in modern style and the Garden of Eden brasserie serves good Dutch food. €€

Bilderberg Hotel Jan Luyken
54–58 Jan Luijkenstraat
Tel: 020-573 0730
Fax: 020-676 3841
www.janluyken.nl
A fine blend of comfort and local character, the Jan Luyken is set in a graceful residential area near the Van Gogh Museum. €€

Bridge
107–11 Amstel
Tel: 020-623 7068
Fax: 020-624 1565
www.thebridgehotel..nl
Overlooking the River Amstel, the Bridge offers space, style and a relaxed atmosphere in its 36 rooms. €€

De Filosoof
6 Anna van den Vondelstraat
Tel: 020-683 3013
Fax: 020-685 3750
www.hotelfilosoof.nl
One of De Filosoof's greatest assets is its location – on a quiet street beside Vondelpark and within walking distance of Leidseplein and the major museums. But its main claim to singularity is its philosophical theme. The individually furnished rooms are inspired by the great thinkers, as is the owner, who is herself a philospher. A haven of comfort and good taste. €€

Die Port Van Cleve
50 Nieuwezijds Voorburgwal
Tel: 020-622 6429
Fax: 020-622 0240
www.dieportvancleve.com
A century-old hotel to the rear of the Royal Palace, with a turreted facade intact and two fine restaurants. €€

Dikker & Thijs Fenice
444 Prinsengracht
Tel: 020-620 1212
Fax: 020-625 8986
www.dtfh.nl
Small, quiet, tasteful and full of character, this gem of a hotel is located adjacent to the busy Leidsestraat shopping street. €€

Keizershof
618 Keizersgracht
Tel: 020-622 2855
Fax: 020-624 8412
www.hotelkeizershof.nl
This wonderful canalside hotel has only six guest rooms, so book as far in advance as possible. The owners, the De Vries family, are most hospitable and take pride in providing a home from home. €€

Right: Die Port Van Cleve, now modernised

Piet Hein
52–53 Vossiusstraat
Tel: 020-662 7205
Fax: 020-662 1526
www.hotelpiethein.nl
Located in a converted mansion in a quiet neighbourhood beside the Vondelpark, the Piet Hein is a popular option offering comfortable rooms. It also has an adjacent annexe. €€

Rembrandt Residence
225 Herengracht
Tel: 020-623 6638
Fax: 020-625 0630
www.rembrandtresidence.nl
A rambling hotel that incorporates a number of old buildings, many of whose original fittings are still in place. Big on atmosphere, less so on modern facilities. €€

Seven Bridges
31 Reguliersgracht
Tel: 020-623 1329
A small, central canal-side hotel with eight rooms plus self-catering apartments in neighbouring houses. The atmosphere is enhanced by well-chosen furnishings and fittings, good views of seven canal bridges and beautiful gardens. €€

Van de Kasteelen
34 Frans van Mierisstraat
Tel: 020-679 8995
Fax: 020-670 6604
www.hotelvandekasteelen.com
The Indonesian family who own and run this hotel, not far from the Concertgebouw, have transformed it into one of the city's simple jewels. There might not be much in the way of luxurious facilities, but all the rooms are clean and offer an adequate level of comfort. €€

Vondel
28–30 Vondelstraat
Tel: 020-612 0120
Fax: 020-685 4321
www.hotelvondel.nl
Comfortable, well-equipped rooms and excellent value for money. Despite its off-centre location, the Vondel is convenient for the Vondelpark and the Leidseplein. €€

Waterfront
458 Singel
Tel/fax: 020-421 6621
www.hotelwaterfront.nl
Typical of the many moderately-priced canal-side hotels, the Waterfront offers atmosphere, comfort and a fair level of service. €€

Winston
125–129 Warmoesstraat
Tel: 020-623 1380
Fax: 020-639 2308
www.winston.nl
Just off the Red-Light District, this has been described as similar to New York's bohemian Chelsea Hotel, attracting artists and musicians. Some rooms are basic and low-priced, while others have been decorated by local artists and are more expensive. €€

Acacia
251 Lindengracht
Tel: 020-622 1460
Fax: 020-638 0748
www.hotelacacia.nl
This fine small hotel in the Jordaan district has plain but comfortable guest rooms and, unusually, a pair of houseboats moored on the adjacent canal. €

Amstel Botel
2–4 Oosterdokskade
Tel: 020-626 4247
Fax: 020-639 1952
www.amstelbotel.com
If you're looking for an offbeat lodging option, try this floating hotel, situated between Centraal Station and the Maritime Museum. The rooms – or cabins – are clean and simple but comfortably furnished with views over the water. Late at night this location is somewhat dubious, so the Amstel Botel is not an ideal choice for single women. €

De Admiraal
563 Herengracht
Tel: 020-626 2150
Fax: 020-623 4625
E-mail: de-admiral-hotel@planet.nl
A friendly, homely hotel, adjacent to the pretty, tree-shaded Thorbeckeplein square, De Admiraal featured in the 1970 Alistair MacLean movie *Puppet on a Chain*. €

practical information

Hoksbergen
301 Singel
Tel: 020-626 6043
Fax: 020-638 3479
www.hotelhoksbergen.com
The Hoksbergen represents an uncommon combination of qualities: high-standard accommodation in a desirable, canal-side location that is good value for money. A characterful, comfortable option. €

Orfeo
12–14 Leidsekruisstraat
Tel: 020-623 1347
Fax: 020-620 2348
www.hotelorfeo.com
Popular with the city's many gay visitors, this hotel just off Leidseplein has simple but clean rooms and a friendly character. The breakfast dining room is a bit bland but Orfeo nevertheless represents good value. €

Parkzicht
33 Roemer Visscherstraat
Tel: 020-618 1954
Fax: 020-618 0897
www.parkzicht.nl
Reasonable rates and a fine location overlooking the Vondelpark are Parkzicht's most pertinent assets, and it is particularly successful in attracting a young clientele. The decor is Old Dutch, while the welcome is friendly. €

Prinsenhof
810 Prinsengracht
Tel: 020-623 1772
Fax: 020-638 3368
www.hotelprinsenhof.com
Although somewhat rough and ready in places, the Prinsenhof is constantly being improved by its enthusiastic owners. The 'casual Amsterdam' atmosphere is what many travellers like about the place. €

Sint Nicolaas
1a Spuistraat
Tel: 020-626 1384
Fax: 020-623 0979
www.hotelnicolaas.nl
This is a friendly, comfortable establishment conveniently located near to Centraal Station. €

Toren
164 Keizersgracht
Tel: 020-622 6352
Fax: 020-626 9705
www.toren.nl
Situated close to Westermarkt, the Toren is a canal-house hotel within two neighbouring buildings. The guest rooms are clean and attractive; most have a private bathroom. €

Van Ostade Bicycle Hotel
123 Van Ostadestraat
Tel: 020-679 3452
Fax: 020-671 5213
www.bicyclehotel.com
The proprietors have turned a commitment to environmentally friendly transport – you can rent bikes cheaply here – into a comfortable hotel for cyclists. €

Wijnnobel
9 *Vossiusstraat*
Tel: 020-662 2298
Small, cheap and cheerful, family-owned hotel with views of the Vondelpark. There are no private bathrooms but the Wijnnobel is conveniently situated, not far from public transport stops, shopping centres and the major museums. €

Budget Hotels & Youth Hostels
Amsterdam has a good array of hostels that are open to guests of all ages. Most offer dormitory accommodation, some provide private rooms, a few have family facilities. Those that require membership can issue you with a card on the spot.

Bob's Youth Hostel
92 Nieuwezijds Voorburgwal
Tel: 020-623 0063
Fax: 020-675 6446
Large, laid-back, middle-of-the-road kind of place, with a good central location and plenty of international fans.

Hans Brinker
136–138 Kerkstraat
Tel: 020-622 0687
Fax: 020-638 2060
www.hans-brinker.com
Fairly clean-cut (no drugs) budget hotel, in a quiet street close to vibrant Leidseplein.

Stayokay Amsterdam Stadsdoelen
97 Kloveniersburgwal
Tel: 020-624 6832
Fax: 020-639 1035
www.stayokay.com
Situated on a canal close to the Red-Light District, a 10-minute walk from the Dam.

Stayokay Amsterdam Vondelpark
5 Zandpad, Vondelpark
Tel: 020-589 8996
Fax: 020-589 8955
www.stayokay.com
A quiet, well-equipped hostel with recreation rooms and a shower and toilet in every room.

Camping
Camping is permitted only on official camp sites. A list of sites is available at VVV offices.

Vliegenbos
138 Meeuwenlaan
Tel: 020-636 8855
Fax: 020-632 2723
www.vliegenbos.nl
In 25 ha (60 acres) of woods, a short ride from the centre. Cabin and tent accommodation.

The following three camp sites are rather inaccessible but the sites' managers will fax directions on request.

De Badhoeve
10 Uitdammerdijk
Tel/fax: 020-490 4294
Gaaspercamping
7 Loosdrechtdreef
Tel: 020-696 7326
Fax: 020-696 9369
www.gaaspercamping-amsterdam.nl
Zeeburg
20 Zuider IJdijk
Tel: 020-694 4430
Fax: 020-694 6238
www.campingzeeburg.nl

HEALTH AND EMERGENCIES

Pharmacies
A list of out-of-hours pharmacies is posted on the front of every *apotheek* (pharmacy).

Medical/Dental Services
In the case of severe accidents, tel: 112. For less urgent cases, standby doctors and dentists can be reached 24 hours a day at the Centraal Doktersdienst, tel: 020-592 3434.

Crime/Trouble
Amsterdam is not particularly violent, but, as is the case in most major Western cities, petty crime is a problem. Exercise caution in the Red-Light District and beware of thieves and pickpockets, especially in crowded areas.

Lost Property
In the case of possessions lost on any city transport, contact the Lost Property Office at 108–114 Prins Hendrikkade, tel: 0900-8011. For items lost on trains or at railway stations, tel: 020-557 8544. The general lost property number is tel: 020-559 3005.

Police
In emergencies, tel: 112.

Toilets
Public toilets are rare. Many restaurant and bar toilets charge a small fee.

COMMUNICATIONS AND NEWS

Post
TPG (post office) opening hours are Mon–Fri 9am–6pm. The post office at 250 Singel is also open Sat 9am–3pm.

Telephone
The country code for The Netherlands is 31. The area code for Amsterdam is 020 from

Right: toddlers of the city unite

elsewhere in the country, 20 from abroad. Card-phones have replaced many coin-operated phones. *Telekaarten* (phone cards) cost €5, €12.50, €25 and €50 from post offices, railway stations and newspaper vendors. To call abroad, dial 00 + country code + area code + subscriber number.

Media

The *International Herald Tribune* and some British broadsheet newspapers are widely available. Cable television offers British and American networks, including the BBC and CNN. BBC Radio 4 can be picked up with good reception on long wave, and the BBC World Service and the Voice of America are both available.

USEFUL INFORMATION

Disabled

Services for disabled people are better than in most European countries. Museums and other public buildings usually have access for wheelchairs. Some trams and the metro network also provide this service.

Children

Amsterdam offers lots of attractions and facilities for children. The following attractions are all relatively child-friendly, depending on the age (and temperament) of the children concerned.

Elektrische Museumtramlijn, Haarlemmermeer Station, 264 Amstelveenseweg, tel: 020-673 7538. For the young tram-spotter.

Holland Experience, 17 Waterlooplein, tel: 020-422 2233. A multimedia introduction to Holland.

Intersphere Laser Games, 194 Prins Hendrikkade, tel: 020-622 4809. Futuristic combat for the older, more macho, child.

Kindermuseum, 2 Linnaeusstraat, tel: 020-568 8233. Part of the Tropenmuseum that is dedicated to children.

Madame Tussaud's, 20 Dam, tel: 020-522 1010. Amsterdam branch of the international institution, featuring waxwork models of famous personalities.

NEMO Science and Technology Centre, 2 Oosterdok, tel: 0900-919 1100. Interactive science museum.

Maps

The pullout map accompanying this book clearly highlights the attractions featured in the itineraries. See also the laminated *Insight Fleximap: Amsterdam* or, for several maps of the city in one, the *Insight Travel Map: Amsterdam*.

The VVV tourist office produces a small map and some hotels provide free maps. You can buy maps at newsagents, book stores and souvenir shops.

Museums

In addition to the museums described in the itineraries, the following might be of interest:

Allard-Pierson Museum (Archaeology), 127 Oude Turfmarkt, tel: 020-525 2556.

Bijbels Museum (The Bible), 366–368 Herengracht, tel: 020-624 2436.

Filmmuseum (Cinema), 3 Vondelpark, tel: 020-589 1400.

Heineken Experience (Brewery), 78 Stadhouderskade, tel: 020-523 9666.

Koffie- en Thee Museum (Coffee and Tea), 67 Warmoesstraat, tel: 020-624 0683.

Museum Amstelkring (Catholic), 40 Oudezijds Voorburgwal, tel: 020-624 6604.

Sexmuseum Amsterdam (Erotica), 18 Damrak, tel: 020-622 8376.

Verzetsmuseum (Resistance Movement), 61 Pantage Kerklaan, tel: 020-620 2535.

Werf 't Kromhout (Shipyard), 147 Hoogte Kadijk, tel: 020-627 6777.

Language

Dutch is spoken everywhere, although there are lots of local dialects, especially in rural areas. The majority of Dutch people speak at least some English, many of them speak it well, and an impressive number are fluent.

SPORT

Bowling

Knijn Bowling, 3 Scheldeplein, tel: 020-664 2211.

Fitness Centres

Fitness Aerobic Centre Jansen, 109–11 Rokin, tel: 020-626 9366.

Sporting Club Zuiderbad, 26 Hobbemastraat, tel: 020-679 2217, tel: 020-620 6631.

Golf

Sloten Golf Course, 1045 Sloterweg, tel: 020-614 2402.
Waterland Golf Course, 141 Buikslotermeerdijk, tel: 020-636 1010.

Ice Skating

Jaap Edenbaan, 64 Radioweg, tel: 020-694 9652.
In winter it is often possible to skate on frozen canals.

Riding

Amsterdamse Manege, 25 Nieuwe Kalfjeslaan, tel: 020-643 1342.

Swimming

Waterlooplein, 28 Valkenburgerstraat, tel: 020-620 6631
De Mirandabad, 9 De Mirandalaan, tel: 020-546 4444.

Tennis

Amstelpark Tenniscentre, 8 Koenenkade, Amsterdamse Bos, tel: 020-301 0700.

Squash

Squash City, Ketelmakerstraat, tel: 020-626 7883.

USEFUL ADDRESSES

Tourist Offices

The VVV (Vereniging voor Vremdelingen Verkeer) local tourism offices are friendly and efficient. VVV Amsterdam has offices at Centraal Station (one inside, by the reservations hall, the other outside on Stationsplein); 1 Leidseplein; and at the corner of Stadionplein. For information from VVV Amsterdam, tel: 0900-400 4040. Netherlands Tourist Information has an office in the arrivals hall of Schiphol Airport. Other tourist offices are:

Haarlem

VVV Zuid-Kennemerland, 1 Stationsplein, tel: 0900-616 1600, fax 023-534 0537, www.vvvzk.nl.

Zandvoort

VVV Zandvoort, 1 Schoolplein, tel: 023-571 7947, fax 023-571 7003, www.vvvzk.nl.

The Hague

VVV Den Haag, 30 Koningin Julianaplein, tel: 0900-340 3505, fax: 070-347 2102, www.denhaag.com.

Scheveningen

VVV Scheveningen, 1134 Gevers Deynootweg, tel: 0900-340 3505, fax: 070-361 5494, www.denhaag.com.

To advance hotel reservations, contact the Netherlands Reservations Centre, 1 Nieuwe Gouw, 1442 LE Purmerend, tel: 0299-689144; fax: 0299-689154; www.hotelres.nl.

City Tours

Artifex (with guides): 342 Herengracht, tel: 020-620 8112.
Yellow Bike (bicycle tours): 29 Nieuwezijds Kolk, tel: 020-620 6940.
Holland International Excursions (throughout Holland): 6 Dam, tel: 020-551 2800.

INSIGHT GUIDES

Insight City Guide: Amsterdam. Indispensible guide to the city with fascinating features, stunning photos and updated travel tips.
Compact Guide: Amsterdam. A handy pocket book with troves of vital information.
Insight Guide: The Netherlands. All facets of the nation are comprehensively and vividly described and illustrated in user-friendly terms.

Above: friendly advice from a VVV office

practical information

www.insightguides.com

✵ INSIGHT GUIDES

The World Leader in Visual Travel Guides & Maps

As travellers become ever more discriminating, Insight Guides is using the vast experience gained over three-and-a-half decades of guide-book publishing to create an even wider range of titles to serve them. For those who want the big picture, Insight Guides and Insight City Guides provide comprehensive coverage of a destination. Insight Pocket Guides supply personal recommendations for a short stay. Insight Compact Guides are attractively portable. Insight FlexiMaps are both rugged and easy to use. And specialist titles cover shopping, eating out, and museums and galleries. Wherever you're going, our writers and photographers have already been there – more than once.

ACKNOWLEDGEMENTS

Photography by

David Beatty/Apa	77
Anne Frank Museum	24B
Guglielmo Galvin/Apa	1, 2/3, 6T, 7T/B, 21, 23, 26T, 28T/B, 29, 30T/B, 31, 34T/B, 36, 39B, 41T/B, 45, 46, 47, 48, 51, 52, 53, 54, 57, 58, 59, 61, 62, 63, 67, 68, 69, 70, 71, 72, 74, 75, 76, 79, 81, 83,84, 86, 89, 91
Rijkmuseum	5, 32
Bill Wassman	6B, 25, 26B, 27, 39T, 42, 43, 44, 60, 64T/B, 65, 73, 80,
Digital Vision/Robert Harding	Cover
Maria Donnelly	Cartography

© APA Publications GmbH & Co. Verlag KG Singapore Branch, Singapore

credits

INDEX

Accommodation 84–89
Aemstelledamme 11
American Hotel 30, 42, 43, 51
Amstel Station 44, 46
Amstel, River 26, 27, 45–46
Amsteldijk 45
Amstelveen Shopping Centre 44
Amstelveen 15
Amsterdam (ship) 12–13, 41
Amsterdam North 40, 61
Amsterdam Stock Exchange 12, 17, 35
Amsterdams Historisch Museum 28
Amsterdamse Waterleidingduinen 60
Amsterdamse Bos (Amsterdam Wood) 49–50
Andrieshofje 48
Anne Frankhuis 15, 24
Archaeological Museum, Haarlem 60
art/artists 13–14, 15, 33
Art Deco 29, 54
Art Nouveau 30, 42, 53
Athenaeum News and Book Centre 28

Bablyon shopping mall, The Hague 63
Bakenesserkerk, Haarlem 58
Bank of Amsterdam 12, 17
bars 52–55
Bartolotti House 24
Beatrix, Queen 14, 17
Beelden aan Zee, Scheveningen 65
beer 11
Begijnhof 28–29
Begijnhof, Haarlem 57–58
Berlage Brug 45
Beurs van Berlage 35
Bezoekerscentrum 50
Bijenkorf (department store) 27
Bird Market 23
Blauwbrug 45
Bloemenmarkt (Flower Market) 25
Blue Gold Fish 25
Bollenstreek (bulb district) 15
Boom Chicago Theater 52
Bosbaan rowing course 50
Botanical Gardens 37–38

Brouwersgracht (Brewers' Canal) 23, 46–7
brown cafés 23, 25, 28, 30, 43, 46, 47, 48, 54, 76
bulb fields 15, 79
Bulldog Palace 51

Calvinism/Calvinists 11, 29, 49
Canal Bike (company) 25, 42
canal boats 21, 29, 40
canals 12, 21, 23–26, 42
casinos 76
Catholics/Catholicism 12, 29, 49
Centraal Station 37, 39–40, 43, 44, 61
cinemas 53, 76
Circuit Park Zandvoort 60
classical music 73–74
COBRA (art movement) 15
COBRA Museum 15
Cobra Museum 44
Comedy Club 51
Concertgebouw 32, 44
Concertgebouw, Haarlem 59
Cycling 21, 45–46, 83

Dam 27
dance 16, 74
De Keyser, Hendrick 23, 24
De Keyser, Pieter 24
De la Mar Theater 42
De Waag 37
Delft pottery 13, 32
Den Haag *(see The Hague)*
diamonds 68
disabled travellers 90
Dockers' strike 15, 17
driving 21, 83
Durgerdam 61

Eating/food 69
ecological site 51
Edam 62
emergencies 89
Erotic Museum 37
Eteresheim 62
events 77

index

Farmers' Market 23
ferries 40, 61
flea market 48
Floris V, Count 11, 17
Floris VI, Count 11
Frank, Anne 15, 17, 24
Frans Hals Museum, Haarlem 59

Gay Pride 16
gays 16, 25, 55
Geological Museum 38
golden age 11–12, 13, 23, 31
government and economy 80
Grand Hotel Krasnapolsky 27
Grand Hotel 36
Grote Kerk, The Hague 64
Grote Markt, Haarlem 59

Haarlem Station 57
Haarlem 57–60
Hague, The 63–65
Hals, Frans 13, 31
Hash Marihuana Hemp Museum 37
hashish 51
health 89
Herengracht (Gentlemen's Canal) 12, 23, 26
Hermitage Amsterdam 45
Het Houten Huys (Wooden House) 29
Holland Casino Amsterdam 30, 43, 51
Holland Casino Zandvoort 60
Holland Experience 49
Holland Festival 16
Holocaust 14, 48
Homomonument 25
Hoorn 62
Hortus Botanicus 37–38
houseboats 23
Houses of Parliament, The Hague 64
Huguenots 12
Huys-Zitten-Weduwe-Hofje 46

IJ Channel 39
IJsselmeer 61
International Court of Justice, The Hague
    65

Jewish Quarter (Jodenbuurt) 48–49
Jewish Resistance Fighters' Memorial 49
Jews 12, 15, 17, 24

Joods Historisch Museum
    48–49
Jordaan 46–48
Juliana, Princess 14

Karthuizerplantsoen 46
Kattenkabinet (Cat Museum) 25–26
Keizersgracht (Emperor's Canal) 12, 23,
    26, 43
Kindermuseum 38
Kleine Gartmanplantsoen 51
Kleine Komedie 53
Koninklijk Paleis (Royal Palace) 27, 43
Kurhaus Hotel, Scheveningen 65

Leidseplein 16, 30, 43, 51–52
Louis Napoleon 14, 17, 27

Madame Tussaud's 27
Madurodam Miniature City,
    The Hague 65
Magna Plaza shoppin
    centre 43
Magere Brug 45
marijuana 51
Marken 62
Martin Luther King
    Park 45
Mata Hari 27
Mauritshuis, The Hague 64
Melkweg 52
merchants' houses 26
Monnickendam 62
Mozes en Aäronkerk 49
Muntplein 25
Munttoren (Mint Tower) 25
Museum Het Rembrandthuis 49
Museum van Loon 26
Museumplein 15, 16, 32
Muziektheater (Opera) 48, 53

Napoleon 14, 17, 27
Nationaal Monument 27
Nazis, invasion 14, 17, 24
NEMO Science and
    Technology Centre 41
Nieuwe Kerk 27, 74
Nieuwmarkt 37
Night Watch, The 14, 31

Noorderkerk 23, 46
Noordermarkt 23, 46

Olympic Stadium 49
Oost-Indisch Huis (East India House) 36
Openluchttheater (Open-Air Theatre) 50
Oude Hoogstraat 36
Oude Kerk 17, 35, 55, 74
Oude Stadhuis, The Hague 64
Ouderkerk aan de Amstel 45
Oudezijds Voorburgwal canal 35, 55

Panorama Mesdag, The Hague 64
patricians' houses 26
Pieter Cornelisz Hooftstraat (PC Hooft)
     34, 43, 44, 67
Planetarium 38
Prinsengracht (Princes' Canal) 12, 23,
     24–25, 43, 47
Purmerend 62

RAI Congresgebouw 44
Red-Light District (Rosse Buurt)
     12, 35–37, 54–5
Rembrandt van Rijn 13–14, 17, 27, 31
Rembrandtplein 29, 53–54
Rijksmuseum 14, 31–32, 43
Roeibaan rowing course 51
Rokin 29
Rosse Buurt (Red-Light District),
     Haarlem 58
Royal Concertgebouw Orchestra
     16, 32

Scharwoude 62
Scheepvaart Museum 12, 41
Scheveningen Sea Life Centre 65
Scheveningen 65
's-Gravenhage *(see The Hague)*
shopping 43, 44, 63, 67–68
Sint-Bavokerk, Haarlem 59
smoking coffee shops 52, 54
Spaarne, River 58
Spiegelgracht 42
Spiegelkwartier (antiques district) 29
sport 91
Spui 28–29
Stadhuis (Town Hall) 48

Stadhuis (Town Hall), Haarlem 60
Stadsschouwburg (City Theatre) 43, 43, 52
Stedelijk Museum 33, 41, 44
Steen, Jan 32

Tasmanstraat 40
Teylers Museum,
     Haarlem 58
Theater Carré 45
Theatermuseum 23
theatre 16, 74
Thorbeckeplein ArtMarket 29
't Lieverdje (sculpture) 28
trams 43–44, 83
Tropenmuseum 38
Tuschinski Theater Cinema 29, 53

United East India Company (Vereenigde
     Oostindische Compagnie/VOC) 12, 17, 36
Utrecht, Bishops of 11, 17
Utrechtse Brug 46

Van Avesnes, Guy, Duke of Hainault 11
Van Gogh Museum 33–34, 44
Van Gogh, Vincent 17, 33, 34 , 44
Van Ruisdael, Jacob 32
Vermeer, Jan 31
Vleeshal, Haarlem 59
Volendam 62
Vondel, Joost van den 27, 34
Vondelpark 16, 34, 43
Vredespaleis (Peace Palace), The Hague 65
Vrije Universiteit Hospital 50
Vrije Universiteit 44

Waalse Kerk, Haarlem 57
Wallen (old town centre)
     12, 35–37
Warder 62
Waterlooplein 46, 48, 49
Westerkerk 25
Westermarkt 25
Willet-Holthuysen Museum 26
World Trade Centre 44, 79

Zandvoort 60
Zeedijk 37
Zuiderzee 11